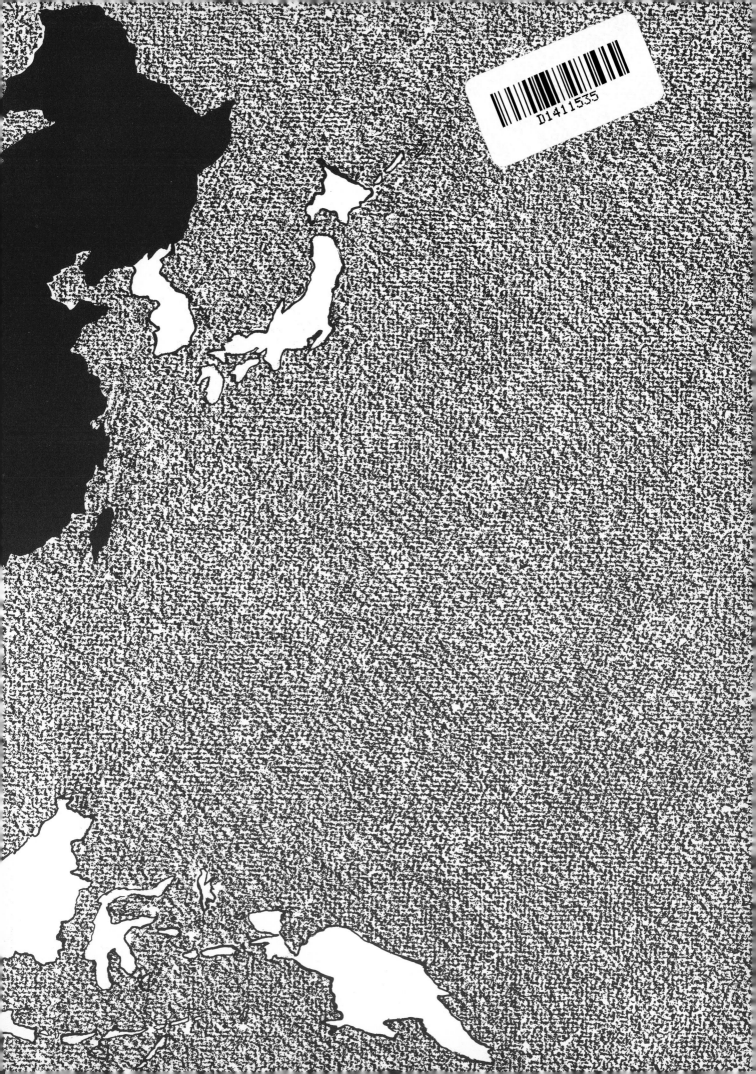

FOODS *of the* ORIENT

Introduced by Sharmini Tiruchelvam

ENIGMA

Picture Credits

Rex Bamber	21, 36, 76, 109
Pat Brindley	108
Patrick Cocklin	106
Alan Duns	19, 51, 56, 64(t), 88, 92, 99, 105
Robert Harding Assoc.	8/9
Paul Kemp	11, 34, 41, 111
David Levin	114
David Meldrum	102
Roger Phillips	10, 13, 14, 26/7, 31, 32/3, 43, 44/5, 49
	53, 58, 63, 64(b), 67, 70, 72, 74, 81, 82/3,
	87, 91, 101, 112
Iain Reid	23, 60, 97
David Smith	39
Sunday Times	7

Edited by Isabel Moore
and Jonnie Godfrey
Published by Marshall Cavendish Books Limited
58 Old Compton Street
London W1V 5PA

© Marshall Cavendish Limited 1978

This volume first published 1978

Printed in Great Britain

ISBN 0 85685 482 4

CONTENTS

INTRODUCTION TO CHINA
Sharmini Tiruchelvam

Good cooking has been an integral part of the brilliant and ancient Chinese culture from the beginning, but it is only comparatively recently that it has been acknowledged outside China as one of the three great 'original' cuisines of the world.

Perhaps that is because it has only been in our own century that most ordinary people in the West have been able to sample even a fraction of the glory of Chinese cooking – although for most of us the 'sampling' could go on for most of our lives for there is a positively bewildering range of dishes, ranging from the almost universally accepted to the downright esoteric!

There are few people today, for instance, who have not tasted or at least heard of Sweet and Sour Pork, Fried Rice, Barbecued Spareribs, Crispy Spring Rolls, Won Tons . . . There are quite a few, too, who know how to make these delicacies at home, for a lot of Chinese cooking is, once one knows how it should look and taste, not at all difficult. Once one has mastered the basic discipline of preparing the food for cooking, it is simplicity itself to do. But of course, there are the rarer gourmet items which could possibly prove more expensive and more difficult to assemble – shark's fin, fish lips, turtle's skirt, bear's paw, sea slugs . . . not to mention the very acquired taste one would need to eat some of them!

Ironically this great heritage originated prior to the days of the sumptuous Courts of Peking and the cosmopolitan elegance of Shanghai in regions of Old China where for one reason or another there was an almost chronic paucity of food. But never was necessity more triumphantly the mother of invention; nothing, absolutely nothing, was wasted. Everything edible (whether from land, fresh water or ocean, or from any part of any animal conventionally despised or ignored) was eaten and combined in several computations with a myriad of other ingredients. Many 'flavours' and textures were created by inventing many different techniques of cooking; the cuisine boasts some 80-odd different ways in all. A few shreds of meat, some diced fresh or dried prawns or shrimps, a handful of cheap chopped vegetables, a touch of garlic, soy or black bean sauce and several minor masterpieces well within the reach of even a poor man were born.

Flavour, texture, quality . . . the Chinese savours each mouthful and is a great connoisseur of his own food. Indeed it is the only way to approach this cuisine oneself: to become swiftly aware of how a dish should look and taste at its best. It is a vitally alive art: adapting, changing sometimes even from its classic origins, to give way to some marvellous new version. Very few taboos operate here, but there are, of course, some basic guidelines; knowledge of the intrinsic qualities of the ingredients being used and of what would best combine with what is still essential.

Cantonese cooking, especially, has stayed close to the Taoist principle that food should be eaten as near to its natural state as possible, with as little cooking and seasoning as possible. Chemical tenderizers such as *vetsin* (monosodium glutamate) are avoided, and cutting and scoring the meats, vegetables and fish in such a way as to achieve the required tenderness preferred. This relies, of course, not only on a knowledge of the 'grain' of the raw materials but also on a knowledge of 'cooking time' and the correct methods of application of heat. A lot of this becomes instinctive after a little practise and one discovers how very little cooking time Chinese food can take. Often a mere dunking in boiling broth or swirling stir-frying in a very little oil will suffice to achieve the required doneness. In today's health-conscious age, this cuisine is among the most enlightened in the world in that easily destroyed precious vitamins are retained intact in the cooked dish.

It is generally held that there are five major schools of Chinese cooking: Canton, Shantung, Schezuan, Fukien and Honan, and two minor ones: Yang Chow and Temple Vegetarian.

Canton
Canton is in southern China, on the coast. A mild climate and access to the sea gave the province a vast variety of foodstuffs and ingredients and it is credited with the invention of the greatest number of dishes – some say around 400,000, with 250 different ways of cooking pork alone!

Cantonese is, however, a no-holds-barred school: practically everything which may be eaten with impunity, from pig's testicles, to snails, frog's legs, fish and chicken heads, ducks' tongues and webbed feet, snakes and sea-urchins, is cooked and eaten. And it is here that the now universally popular *Dim Sum* originated.

Literally translated, *Dim Sum* means 'something to dot the heart with.' Traditionally a tea-house repast, many Chinese restaurants today will keep the *Dim Sum* trays – tiers of steaming bamboo baskets piled high over boiling water or bouillon, with those items needing the least cooking at the very top – coming from morning until evening. Mouth-sized morsels of delicious, steamed spare-ribs in sauce, called *Thai Kuat*; red-cooked sweet-savoury pork in cloud-light white buns called *Char Siew Pau*; and a magically successful combination of diced pork and crisp, sliced water-chestnuts wrapped in the merest skin of egg-dough topped with crab's eggs, called *Siew Mai*, are among the classic array of low-calorie, steamed, high-protein snacks suitable for eating from morning until cocktail time.

Cantonese cooking also specializes in soups, especially turtle soup, steamed, roasted and grilled (broiled) pork and poultry dishes; 'double-pan' and large earthenware casserole-type cooking. A great deal of clear chicken broth is used as a stock or base for light gravies and is preferred to the sugar used by other schools to achieve 'sweetness'. And, of course, in keeping with the Taoist principle, underdone is well done, literally, in Canton! This is particularly true of their low-oil, quick, stir-fried 'chow' dishes, a technique which originated in Yang Chow; hence the name.

Shantung
Shantung is the northernmost of all the different schools with Peking perhaps the best known city which follows this style of cooking. It has nothing like the range or variety of Canton but is famous for a handful of wondrous dishes like Fragrant and Crispy Peking Duck and Duck Soup.

This area is specially noted for its 'drunken' dishes – i.e. dishes marinated or cooked in wines, such as swan's liver. Although the cooking is not heavy, on the whole the sauces are richer than those of Canton. Flavouring is heavier, with light and dark soy, with the accent on the latter, crushed garlic, black and red bean pastes and sauces. Plum sauce is another favourite accompaniment. Wheat, not rice, is the staple of the north and dumplings and noodles made from it are cooked in every conceivable way, and combined with pork, seafood, poultry, offal (variety meat) and vegetables.

History plays a great part; for the Mongols came and ruled here, and brought with them their techniques of marinating and barbecueing meats. The Mongolian Hot Pot is obviously the ancestor of the modern Firepot: a dish where each diner can cook his own food in a central hot-pot, dipping into a variety of sauces and ladling a little of the soup into his own individual bowl. And the Mongols also left their taste for dairy produce and mutton, much disliked by the rest of China. The five-spice mixture of anise, cinnamon, cloves, fennel and star anise is used as a seasoning.

Szechuan
In the western part of the central province is a vast basin of luxuriant vegetation, bounded by mountain ranges and densely populated: Szechuan.

Szechuan is famous for its spicy, piquant dishes; for its fungi, particularly truffles, and for the subtlety of its 'hot', multi-flavoured cuisine. It is also known as the site of the Chinese equivalent of Camelot!

The preponderance of hot spicy food has its roots in history. Only one great crop was produced each year, and in order to ensure an adequate supply of food the year round, they took to preserving their produce. The humidity precluded sun-drying or salting (both popular on the coast) and so spicing was used instead. They made chilli and peppercorn pastes, fermented rice, made wine vinegar and added a fair bit of brown sugar. All of which resulted in a series of fascinating savoury-hot, hot-sour-spiced, sweet-sour and sweet-hot-sharp dishes.

One of those dishes is *Yu Hsiang Jou si*, succulent pork strips stir-fried with what are called 'spicy' fish ingredients and fungi. Another is beef, carrots and peppers cut into strips and fried crisp, with chillis. This school also specializes in paper-wrapped cooking of poultry and various meats.

The fungi which grow in Szechuan are particularly delicious. And like nearby Yunan – which is famous rather like Parma in Italy for just one thing: ham – it also specializes in preserving meats by curing and smoking them. Its dishes tend to be more oily than those of the other schools.

Fukien
Fukien is very much a specialist school. It has none of the variety of Canton or Szechuan, but it is noted for the quality and lightness of its cooking, specializing in clear and tasty soups. Indeed, there are those who would fault it on this basis, saying that most Fukien dishes are perhaps too soupy. Fukien is famous for the quality of its soy sauce and for red-cooked dishes – meat or vegetables cooked or braised in a soy sauce-based liquid. The province has a long sea coast and seafood is therefore very popular, and what cannot be used in any one season is salted and sun dried for the next. Dried scallops form the basis of some of the best soups of the region, and have a unique and unforgettably delicate flavour.

During a short break from work, Chinese workers drink tea on the historic Great Wall of China.

6

Honan

Like Shantung, Honan was once the capital, the seat of a great court. Like Szechuan it grows the most wondrous fungi.

It was the cooks of Honan who first produced one of China's best-known flavours: the sweet-sour sauce. And it is they who devised a dip-fry method using boiling oil to cook ingredients like kidneys which shrink greatly on cooking through loss of moisture. The Honan method of dip-frying consists of intermittently dipping then removing the food from boiling oil, and results in a delicate balance between a crisp sealed outside and a tender-textured inside all at once.

Yang Chow

The Yangtze river bisects China, running from west to east. At its easternmost end, where it empties its great self into the magical-sounding China Sea, stands the luminous city of Shanghai. Claimed to be the most cosmopolitan of the great centres of cooking, it has its roots in the classic cooking of the school of Yang Chow.

Yang Chow was formerly a salt-rich mining city full of wealthy merchants and together the two cities stood at the easternmost end of the Yangtze. Yang Chow had all the advantages of wealth, of access to the sea and its produce, and to the fruits of the fertile valley of the river. The cooks of Yang Chow specialized in a wide range of cooking from long slow-cooking casseroles to light, airy, swiftly prepared snacks.

Access to the salt-trading post of Ningpo, also close by, which specialized in lightly spiced and steamed foods, and the availability of fresh sea-foods, greatly added to its own repertoire. They too, turned into a great art, sun-drying, salting, smoking and curing, and specialized in spicing and preserving seafoods such as squid and prawns (shrimp). They were among the first to combine both the fresh and the dried variety of the same ingredient in the same dish – an idea now copied by much of the rest of South East Asia.

Two dishes from Yang Chow have been adopted by all the schools of cooking and are now regarded as national dishes: *Chow Mein* and *Chow Fan*. In short they originated Fried Noodles and Fried Rice . . . and the all-important technique of 'Chow' cooking. Chow cooking – that is low-oil, quick stir-frying came originally from Yang Chow. (Ironically, however, it was Canton which went on to exploit it best.) But in time Shanghai grew and surpassed and eclipsed Yang Chow in power, fame and sophistication; so much so that, apart from a few who know how much Chinese cooking owes to the school of Yang Chow, it has faded from memory, and is today regarded as only a minor school, with Canton and Shanghai receiving the credit for many Yang Chow masterpieces.

The Vegetarian School

The Buddhist temples of China adhered very strictly to a vegetarian diet. Today the West is discovering with interest this particular school of cooking.

The Chinese on the whole dislike dairy products, but obviously if both dairy products and meat are removed from the diet a substitute is necessary for properly balanced nutrition. In all of China, and emanating from this style of cooking, that substitute is the soy bean. It reigns supreme, taking not only the place of dairy products but indeed of every meat and fish under the sun. For such is the consummate knowledge of cooking it that almost every conceivable type of dish has been made out of every part of the soy plant – milk, curd, 'cheese', cake and sprouts, in marvellous imitation of the texture, flavour and shape of meat and fish so as to be (almost) indistinguishable from them. Sautéed soy bean curd is produced to taste and look in turn like delicate calves' brains or the fluffiest omelette.

Preparation

There is no doubt that the bulk of the 'work' of Chinese cooking lies in assembly and preparation. A basic part of this preparation is the cutting up of food, and, to get the best results, some knowledge of the 'grain' of the meats and vegetables are required. There are five main types of cutting: dicing, slicing, chopping, oblique-cutting and shredding. To watch a Chinese cook deftly wielding a Chinese chopper at speed is to watch the performance of an artist. But they do say that, although it does look unwieldy and far more difficult to use than a sharp knife, once one gets the hang of it, it is far easier to use!

Techniques of Cooking

The Chinese claim to have evolved some 80-odd techniques of cooking and combining foods. Some of these, of course, are the ordinary ones known to every Western cook and housewife, such as steaming and boiling, and some are refinements and

Water buffaloes are traditionally used in agriculture to plough rice-paddies.

variations of those methods. Some of them are, however, unique to Chinese cooking. 'Stir-frying' for instance is a form of swift, light sautéeing where the food is kept constantly in motion so that every morsel is evenly and swiftly cooked. The ubiquitous *wok*, a sort of frying-pan with gently sloping sides, is best for this type of cooking, especially when used with wooden cooking chopsticks (which are longer than eating ones). Red-cooking is also uniquely Chinese and is not a slang expression denoting political leanings, but rather a method of cooking a whole range of meat, poultry, game and fish dishes, in soy sauce, resulting in a lovely, rich red glaze to the food. Meats cooked like this, especially, will keep well and combine well later – hot or cold – with other ingredients.

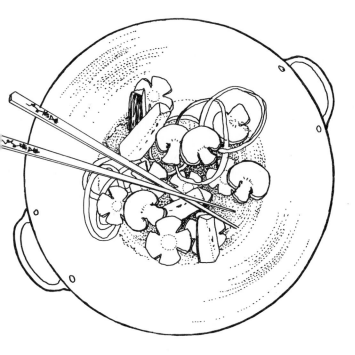

(Left) The Chinese chopper and shredder are essential tools in the preparation of Chinese food.

(Below) The wok is the traditional cooking utensil in China and is ideal for stir-frying.

Eating Chinese

Without doubt part of the fun of cooking Chinese is to serve and eat Chinese.

Setting: The classic Chinese table is usually round because dishes are traditionally brought in one at a time, diners helping themselves from a common central dish, and it is important that each guest be an equal distance from the central dish.

Each place setting has bowls, a china spoon, chopsticks, saucers. Condiments are set out: usually vinegar and soy sauce in pourers and chilli sauce, chilli oil and mustard sauce in saucers.

Etiquette: Etiquette decrees that each diner reaches for food from the central dish, serving himself with his own chopsticks from that part of the dish facing him. Perfect politeness also decrees that he should endeavour not to let the chopsticks touch his mouth and that he picks up every piece of food that his chopsticks touch from the main dish. When laying down one's chopsticks never cross them. That is taken by many Chinese to be the height of bad manners and even of enmity, for they believe crossed chopsticks to be a sign of ill-luck for the host.

Tea: Hot tea without milk or sugar is the usual accompaniment to a Chinese meal unless wine or spirits are being drunk.

Tea is usually drunk between dishes to cleanse the palate. It also has a social and ceremonial function and is said to be 'healthy', dissolving the grease in the food and washing it through the system and away. Curiously, in hot weather the tea induces a gentle pleasant sweating and thereby cools the body. In the winter it warms it. Certain herbal teas also have a medicinal value and are meant to be very good for the liver and the kidneys – quite apart from the delicate aroma and delicious flavours. Vanity too is served here, for some of them are supposed to be good for the complexion and for the brightness of the whites of the eyes. So they say.

Wine: Warmed sake with hot weak tea as a chaser makes a good winter accompaniment, but for those purists who would like to stay with Chinese wines here is the briefest resumé:

Gao Liang, from northern China, is a rice wine somewhat stronger than vodka or gin. More suitable for winter than summer. *Shao Hsing*, from central China, is a rather milder, sweeter, yellowish wine also made from rice. This is by far the most popular wine to drink while eating. *Liao Pan* – whose literal translation means 'half-strength' – is an orange blossom or green plum wine from south China. It is usually very mild and pleasant, although there are more potent forms of it: you will only discover the strength by tasting each jar or bottle as it comes!

Some Final Thoughts

The garnishing and presentation of food is as much an art with the Chinese as the cooking of it. The 'look of it' is important from a point of view of colour, form and imagination. The 'placing' of the dish within the order of the menu is another grace note, for unlike an Indian meal where everything is served at once these dishes, to be appreciated fully, should be served one at a time and each should act as an appetizer to the next.

The naming of dishes, too, makes the imagination soar back into the mists of the romantic past: Gold Coin; Eight-Jewel Duck; Splashed Shrimps; Red-Cooked Lion's Head. There is always a story. Like the one about the Emperor Chien-lung wandering incognito into an inn in search of a meal. The innkeeper, clean out of food but unwilling to disappoint anyone at all, remembers that he has a piece of crusty, near-burned rice at the bottom of his empty pot of cooked rice. He fishes it out and ingeniously uses part of it to make a rice broth and uses part of the toasty rice as a biscuit to serve with the broth! The Emperor was so taken with this unique dish that he ordered his own chefs to discover how this was made. Through experiments they produced its equivalent, the dish which is today known as *Gaw Bar* and is a classic part of the Chinese repertoire.

So now read on, sample and delight in the wonders of an ancient, yet very modern cuisine.

SOUPS & DIM SUM

Birds' Nest Soup

Metric/Imperial	American
4 birds' nests	4 birds' nests
1.5 l./2½ pints chicken stock	6¼ cups chicken stock
salt and pepper to taste	salt and pepper to taste
125g./4oz. cooked chicken, finely shredded	½ cup finely shredded cooked chicken
4 slices of ham, finely chopped	4 slices of ham, finely chopped
¼ tsp. monosodium glutamate (optional)	¼ tsp. M.S.G. (optional)

Soak the nests for 12 hours in warm water, changing the water once or twice during the period. Remove any protruding feathers with tweezers.

Pour the stock into a large saucepan and bring to the boil. Season to taste and drop in the birds' nests. Cover the pan, reduce the heat to low and simmer for 20 minutes. Stir in the remaining ingredients and simmer for a further 1 minute.

Pour into a warmed tureen and serve.

Serves 4
Preparation and cooking time: 12½ hours

Wonton Soup

Metric/Imperial	American
½kg./1lb. lean pork or beef, minced	1lb. lean pork or beef, ground
2 Tbs. soya sauce	2 Tbs. soy sauce
2.5cm/1in. piece of fresh root ginger, peeled and finely chopped	1in. piece of fresh green ginger, peeled and finely chopped
1 tsp. salt	1 tsp. salt
1 tsp. grated nutmeg	1 tsp. grated nutmeg
275g./10oz. chopped spinach	1½ cups chopped spinach
225g./8oz. wonton dough (see page 39) thinly rolled and cut into 36 squares, or 36 bought wonton wrappers	8oz. wonton dough (see page 39) thinly rolled and cut into 36 squares, or 36 bought wonton wrappers
1.75l./3 pints chicken stock	2 quarts chicken stock
1 bunch of watercress, chopped	1 bunch of watercress, chopped

Put the pork or beef, soy sauce, ginger, salt, nutmeg and spinach in a bowl and mix thoroughly.

Lay the wonton squares or wrappers on a flat surface. Put a little filling just below the centre and wet the edges of the dough. Fold one corner of the dough over the filling to make a triangle and pinch the edges together to seal. Pull the corners at the base together and pinch to seal.

Half-fill a large saucepan with water and bring to the boil. Drop in the wontons and return to the boil. Cook for 5 minutes, or until the wontons are tender but still firm.

Remove from the heat and pour off the water. Return the wontons to the pan and pour in the stock. Bring to the boil, then add the watercress. Return to the boil and transfer to a warmed tureen before serving.

Serves 6
Preparation and cooking time: 20 minutes

Hot and Sour Soup

Wonton Soup contains delicious wonton triangles stuffed with pork or beef and spinach.

Metric/Imperial	American
2 Tbs. sesame oil	2 Tbs. sesame oil
2 medium onions, finely chopped	2 medium onion, finely chopped
2 Tbs. flour	2 Tbs. flour
1.2 l./2 pints chicken stock	5 cups chicken stock
1 Tbs. lemon juice	1 Tbs. lemon juice
2 Tbs. soya sauce	2 Tbs. soy sauce
salt and pepper to taste	salt and pepper to taste
275g./10oz. bean sprouts	1¼ cups bean sprouts
2 dried mushrooms, soaked in cold water for 30 minutes, drained and chopped	2 dried mushrooms, soaked in cold water for 30 minutes, drained and chopped
125g./4oz. tin water chestnuts drained and chopped	4oz. can water chestnuts, drained and chopped
125g./4oz. crabmeat, diced	½ cup diced crabmeat

Heat the oil in a heavy saucepan. When it is hot, add the onions and cook, stirring occasionally, until they are soft. Remove the pan from the heat and stir in the flour to make a smooth paste. Gradually add the stock, then stir in the lemon juice, soy sauce, salt, pepper, bean sprouts, mushrooms, water chestnuts and crabmeat. Return the pan to moderate heat and bring to the boil, stirring constantly. Cover then simmer for 1 hour. Transfer to a warmed tureen and serve.
Serves 6
Preparation and cooking time: 1½ hours.

13

Tsingshih Ham and Cucumber Soup

Metric/Imperial	American
2 large cucumbers, peeled and cubed	2 large cucumbers, peeled and cubed
2 dried mushrooms, soaked in cold water for 30 minutes, drained and chopped	2 dried mushrooms, soaked in cold water for 30 minutes, drained and chopped
900ml./1½ pints chicken stock	3¾ cups chicken stock
salt and pepper to taste	salt and pepper to taste
225g./8oz. smoked ham, finely chopped	1 cup finely chopped smoked ham

Put the cucumbers and mushrooms into a large saucepan and add the stock and seasoning. Bring to the boil. Cover the pan, reduce the heat to low and simmer the soup for 20 minutes. Stir in the ham and simmer for a further 5 minutes.

Transfer to a warmed tureen and serve.

Serves 4
Preparation and cooking time: 1 hour

Yu-chi Tang

(Shark's Fin Soup)

This dish is one of the great delicacies of China, and is often served on special occasions. It is traditionally accompanied by a small bowl of cooked bamboo shoots.

Metric/Imperial	American
2 Tbs. sesame oil	2 Tbs. sesame oil
1 spring onion, finely chopped	1 scallion, finely chopped
2.5cm./1in. piece of fresh root ginger, peeled and finely chopped	1in. piece of fresh green ginger, peeled and finely chopped
4 dried mushrooms, soaked in cold water for 30 minutes, drained and thinly sliced	4 dried mushrooms, soaked in cold water for 30 minutes, drained and thinly sliced
2 Tbs. rice wine or dry sherry	2 Tbs. rice wine or dry sherry
2l./3½ pints chicken stock	2¼ quarts chicken stock
125g./4oz. ready-prepared shark's fin, soaked for 1 hour in cold water and drained	½ cup ready-prepared shark's fin, soaked for 1 hour in cold water and drained
225g./8oz. boned chicken breast, shredded	1 cup boned shredded chicken breast
225g./8oz. shelled small shrimps	1⅓ cups peeled small shrimp
1½ Tbs. soya sauce	1½ Tbs. soy sauce
1½ Tbs. cornflour, mixed to a paste with 1 Tbs. chicken stock	1½ Tbs. cornstarch, mixed to a paste with 1 Tbs. chicken stock

Heat the oil in a saucepan. When it is hot, add the spring onion (scallion), ginger, mushrooms and rice wine or sherry and fry, stirring occasionally, for 5 minutes. Add half the stock and the shark's fin and bring to the boil. Simmer for 10 minutes, then add the chicken, shrimps and soy sauce. Pour in the remaining stock and cornflour (cornstarch) mixture and bring to the boil, stirring. Simmer for 10 minutes, stirring occasionally.

Pour into a warmed tureen and serve.

Serves 8-10
Preparation and cooking time: 1½ hours

No important feast or dinner can pass without serving Yu-Chi-Tang (Shark's Fin Soup), one of China's most famous delicacies.

Egg Drop Soup

Metric/Imperial	American
1 Tbs. vegetable oil	1 Tbs. vegetable oil
1 medium onion, thinly sliced	1 medium onion, thinly sliced
1 small cucumber, finely diced	1 small cucumber, finely diced
1.75l./3 pints chicken stock	2 quarts chicken stock
4 medium tomatoes, quartered	4 medium tomatoes, quartered
1 egg, lightly beaten	1 egg, lightly beaten

Heat the oil in a large saucepan. When it is hot, add the onion and fry for 1 minute, stirring constantly. Add the cucumber and fry for 1 minute. Stir in the stock and bring it to the boil. Reduce the heat to low and simmer for 10 minutes, stirring occasionally. Stir in the tomato quarters and simmer very gently for a further 5 minutes.

Remove the pan from the heat and using a whisk or fork, carefully whisk the egg into the soup.

Serve at once.

Serves 6
Preparation and cooking time: 25 minutes

Watercress and Pork Soup

Metric/Imperial	American
6 dried mushrooms, soaked in cold water for 30 minutes and drained	6 dried mushrooms, soaked in cold water for 30 minutes and drained
½kg./1lb. pork fillets, cut into thin strips	1lb. pork tenderloin, cut into thin strips
2 bunches of watercress, chopped	2 bunches of watercress, chopped
1.75l./3 pints chicken stock	2 quarts chicken stock
2 celery stalks, cut into strips	2 celery stalks, cut into strips
2 carrots, cut into thin strips	2 carrots, cut into thin strips
6 spring onions, chopped	6 scallions, chopped
1 tsp. salt	1 tsp. salt
1 tsp. sugar	1 tsp. sugar
½ tsp. white pepper	½ tsp. white pepper
1 Tbs. soya sauce	1 Tbs. soy sauce

Remove the stalks from the mushrooms then cut the mushroom caps into thin strips and set aside.

Put the pork and watercress into a large saucepan and pour over the stock. Bring to the boil. Reduce the heat to low and simmer the soup for 20 minutes. Stir in all the remaining ingredients and bring to the boil. Simmer the soup for a further 5 minutes.

Pour into a warmed tureen and serve at once.

Serves 6-8
Preparation and cooking time: 1 hour

Chicken and Sweetcorn Soup

Metric/Imperial	American
3 Tbs. vegetable oil	3 Tbs. vegetable oil
4cm./1½in. piece of fresh root ginger, peeled and chopped	1½in. piece of fresh green ginger, peeled and chopped
125g./4oz. cooked chicken meat, finely chopped	⅔ cup finely chopped cooked chicken meat
4 dried mushrooms, soaked in cold water for 30 minutes, drained and stalks removed	4 dried mushrooms, soaked in cold water for 30 minutes, drained and stalks removed
400g./14oz. tin sweetcorn, drained	14oz. can sweetcorn, drained
600ml./1 pint chicken stock	2½ cups chicken stock
1 tsp. salt	1 tsp. sugar
2 tsp. cornflour, mixed to a paste with 1 Tbs. water	2 tsp. cornstarch, mixed to a paste with 1 Tbs. water

Heat the oil in a large saucepan. When it is hot, add the ginger and stir-fry for 2 minutes. Add the chicken meat and stir-fry for 2 minutes. Chop the mushrooms if they are large, then stir them into the pan with the sweetcorn. Pour over the stock and sugar. Bring to the boil, reduce the heat to low and simmer the soup for 10 minutes.

Stir in the cornflour (cornstarch) mixture until the liquid thickens slightly and becomes translucent. Serve at once.

Serves 4
Preparation and cooking time: 30 minutes

Wontons with Pork

Metric/Imperial	American
225g./8oz. lean pork, minced	8oz. lean pork, ground
2 tsp. rice wine or dry sherry	2 tsp. rice wine or dry sherry
2 tsp. soya sauce	2 tsp. soy sauce
1 tsp. salt	1 tsp. salt
1 tsp. sugar	1 tsp. sugar
2 tsp. cornflour	2 tsp. cornstarch
1 Chinese or savoy cabbage leaf, chopped	1 Chinese or savoy cabbage leaf, chopped
3 water chestnuts, finely chopped	3 water chestnuts, finely chopped
1 spring onion, finely chopped	1 scallion, finely chopped
225g./8oz. wonton dough (see page 39), thinly rolled and cut into 36 squares, or 36 bought wonton wrappers	8oz. wonton dough (see page 39) thinly rolled and cut into 36 squares, or 36 bought wonton wrappers

Put the pork, wine or sherry, soy sauce, salt, sugar and cornflour (cornstarch) into a bowl and knead gently to blend. Beat in the cabbage, water chestnuts and spring onion (scallion).

Lay the wonton squares or wrappers on a flat surface. Put a little filling just below the centre and wet the edges of the dough. Fold one corner of the dough over the filling to make a triangle and pinch the edges together to seal. Pull the corners at the base together and pinch to seal. Repeat this process until all the wonton wrappers are filled and sealed.

Half-fill a large saucepan or the bottom of a steamer with water and bring to the boil. Place the wontons in a heatproof bowl on the top half of the steamer and wontons should be arranged in one layer). Steam the wontons for 30 minutes.

Transfer to a warmed serving dish and serve piping hot.

Serves 6-8

Preparation and cooking time: 1½ hours (if cooking in two batches)

Wontons with Pork and Prawn or Shrimps

Metric/Imperial	American
2 Tbs. vegetable oil	2 Tbs. vegetable oil
225g./8oz. lean pork, minced	8oz. lean pork, ground
225g./8oz. peeled prawns, finely chopped	1⅓ cups finely chopped peeled shrimps
2 Tbs. soya sauce	2 Tbs. soy sauce
1 Tbs. rice wine or dry sherry	1 Tbs. rice wine or dry sherry
½ tsp. salt	½ tsp. salt
5 bamboo shoots, finely chopped	5 bamboo shoots, finely chopped
2 dried mushrooms, soaked in cold water for 30 minutes, drained and chopped	2 dried mushrooms, soaked in cold water for 30 minutes, drained and chopped
2 spring onions, finely chopped	2 scallions, finely chopped
1 tsp. cornflour, mixed to a paste with 1 Tbs. water	1 tsp. cornstarch, mixed to a paste with 1 Tbs. water
225g./8oz. wonton dough (see page 39), thinly rolled and cut into 36 squares, or 36 bought wonton wrappers	8oz. wonton dough (see page 39), thinly rolled and cut into 36 squares, or 36 bought wonton wrappers
vegetable oil for deep-frying	vegetable oil for deep-frying

Heat the oil in a frying-pan. When it is hot, add the pork and fry until it loses its pinkness. Stir in the prawns or shrimp, rice wine or sherry, soy sauce, salt, bamboo shoots, mushrooms and spring onions (scallions) and fry for 1 minute, stirring constantly. Stir in the cornflour (cornstarch) mixture until the pan mixture thickens. Remove from the heat and transfer the mixture to a bowl. Set aside to cool.

Lay the wonton squares or wrappers on a flat surface. Put a little filling just below the centre and wet the edges of the dough. Fold one corner of the dough over the filling to make a triangle and pinch the edges together to seal. Pull the corners at the base together and pinch to seal. Repeat this process until all the wonton wrappers are filled and sealed.

Fill a large saucepan one-third full with oil and heat until it is hot. Carefully lower the wontons into the oil, a few at a time, and fry for 2 to 3 minutes, or until they are golden brown. Remove from the oil and drain on kitchen towels.

Transfer the wontons to a warmed serving dish and serve hot.

Serves 6-8

Preparation and cooking time: 1 hour

Hsia Jen Tu Ssu

(Shrimp Toast)

Wontons have a marvellous variety of fillings and can be served as an hors d'oeuvre, as part of a main meal or as a sweet.

Metric/Imperial	American
225g./8oz. peeled shrimps	1⅓ cups peeled shrimp
25g./1oz. lean salt pork, blanched in boiling water for 5 minutes to remove excess salt	1oz. lean salt pork, blanched in boiling water for 5 minutes to remove excess salt
2 Tbs. rice wine or dry sherry	2 Tbs. rice wine or dry sherry
salt and white pepper to taste	salt and white pepper to taste
2 egg whites, beaten until frothy	2 egg whites, beaten until frothy
2 Tbs. cornflour	2 Tbs. cornstarch
1 tsp. very finely chopped parsley	1 tsp. very finely chopped parsley
1 egg, lightly beaten	1 egg, lightly beaten
10-12 thin slices of white bread, cut into rounds, squares or triangles	10-12 thin slices of white bread, cut into rounds, squares or triangles
vegetable oil for deep-frying	vegetable oil for deep-frying

Put the shrimps and salt pork in a dish and chop and pound them together until they are pulpy. Beat in the wine or sherry, seasoning, egg whites, half the cornflour (cornstarch) and parsley until the mixture forms a thick paste. Alternatively, put all the above ingredients in a blender and purée until smooth.

Beat the remaining cornflour (cornstarch) and egg together, then lightly brush the mixture over the bread shapes. Spread the shrimp paste over the bread shapes.

Fill a large saucepan one-third full with oil and heat until very hot. Carefully lower the shrimp toasts into the oil, a few at a time, and fry for about 3 minutes, shrimp side up. (You may have to use a slotted spoon to keep the toasts this side up.) Turn over and fry for a further 3 minutes on the other side, or until they are deep golden brown and crisp. Remove from the oil and drain thoroughly on kitchen towels. Serve piping hot.

Serves 6-8
Preparation and cooking time: 40 minutes

Chinese Spareribs

Metric/Imperial	American
1kg./2lb. American-style spareribs, cut into individual ribs	2lb. spareribs, cut into individual ribs
1 tsp. salt	1 tsp. salt
4 Tbs. peanut oil	4 Tbs. peanut oil
2 garlic cloves, crushed	2 garlic cloves, crushed
½ small onion, finely chopped	1 small onion, finely chopped
4cm./1½in. piece of fresh root ginger, peeled and finely chopped	1½in. piece of fresh green ginger, peeled and finely chopped
4 Tbs. soya sauce	4 Tbs. soy sauce
3 Tbs. dry sherry	3 Tbs. dry sherry
1 Tbs. castor sugar	1 Tbs. superfine sugar
black pepper to taste	black pepper to taste
150ml./5fl.oz. chicken stock	⅔ cup chicken stock

Rub the spareribs all over with salt. Heat the oil in a large frying pan. When the oil is very hot, add the garlic, onion and ginger. Stir-fry for 1 minute. Add the ribs, reduce the heat slightly and stir-fry for a further 5 minutes. Remove the ribs from the pan. Stir the soy sauce, sherry, sugar and pepper into the pan and stir-fry for 2 minutes. Return the ribs to the pan.

Pour in the stock and turn the ribs so that they are well coated. Reduce the heat to low and simmer for 5 minutes. Cover and leave to simmer gently for 20 minutes. Remove the lid. Turn the ribs, re-cover and continue to simmer for 10 minutes.

Preheat the oven to fairly hot 190°C (Gas Mark 5, 375°F). Arrange the ribs in a roasting pan and spoon over any remaining sauce. Put into the oven for 5-10 minutes, or until the surface of the ribs is dry and crisp. Serve at once.
Serves 4
Preparation and cooking time: 1 hour

Dumplings with Crab Meat

Metric/Imperial	American
6 dried mushrooms, soaked in cold water for 30 minutes and drained	6 dried mushrooms, soaked in cold water for 30 minutes and drained
2 Tbs. sesame oil	2 Tbs. sesame oil
1 Tbs. chopped spring onion	1 Tbs. chopped scallion
1 tsp. finely chopped fresh root ginger	1 tsp. finely chopped fresh green ginger
225g./8oz. crabmeat, shell and cartilage removed and flaked	8oz. crabmeat, shell and cartilage removed and flaked
salt and pepper to taste	salt and pepper to taste
¼ tsp. sugar	¼ tsp. sugar
1 tsp. soya sauce	1 tsp. soy sauce
1 Tbs. sherry	1 Tbs. sherry
DUMPLINGS	DUMPLINGS
225g./8oz. flour	2 cups flour
125ml./4.floz. boiling water	½ cup boiling water

Cut off the mushroom stalks and chop the caps finely.

Heat the oil in a frying-pan. When the oil is very hot, add the spring onion (scallion), ginger, mushrooms and crabmeat and stir-fry for 3 minutes over moderately high heat.

Stir in the salt, pepper, sugar, soy sauce and sherry and stir-fry for a further 1 minute. Remove from the heat and set aside.

Sift the flour into a bowl, then gradually pour in the water, mixing until all the flour is incorporated and the dough comes away from the sides of the bowl. Cover with a cloth and set aside for 30 minutes.

Roll out the dough into a sausage about 2.5cm./1in. in diameter, then cut into slices about 2.5cm./1in. wide. Flatten the slices until they are about 7.5cm./3in. in diameter.

Put a teaspoonful of the crabmeat mixture on one side of each circle, then fold over to make a semi-circle. Seal the edges by pinching them together.

Half-fill a large saucepan with water and bring to the boil.

Put the dumplings in a heatproof bowl or the top half of a steamer and place over the boiling water. (If the dumplings will not fit in the bowl in one layer, steam them in two batches.)

Cover and steam the dumplings for 10 minutes. Serve hot.

Serves 4
Preparation and cooking time: 1½ hours

Chinese Spareribs are made with individual American style ribs stir-fried in a delicious mixture of sherry, soy sauce, sugar and pepper.

NOODLES, RICE & FOO YUNG

Lo Mein

(Beef and Vegetables with Noodles)

Metric/Imperial	American
225g./8oz. rump steak, cut across the grain into thin strips	8oz. rump steak, cut across the grain into thin strips
4 Tbs. oyster sauce	4 Tbs. oyster sauce
125ml./4fl.oz. sesame oil	$\frac{1}{2}$ cup sesame oil
350g./12oz. egg noodles or spaghetti	12oz. egg noodles or spaghetti
4 dried mushrooms, soaked in cold water for 30 minutes, drained and sliced	4 dried mushrooms, soaked in cold water for 30 minutes, drained and sliced
125g./4oz. bamboo shoots, finely chopped	$\frac{1}{2}$ cup finely chopped bamboo shoots
225g./8oz. Chinese cabbage, shredded	$1\frac{1}{3}$ cups shredded Chinese cabbage
225g./8oz. bean sprouts	1 cup bean sprouts
1 tsp. soft brown sugar	1 tsp. soft brown sugar
2 Tbs. soya sauce	2 Tbs. soy sauce
2 spring onions, chopped	2 scallions, chopped
125ml./4fl.oz. beef stock	$\frac{1}{2}$ cup beef stock

Put the meat strips into a shallow bowl. Pour over 3 tablespoons of the oyster sauce and 1 tablespoon of sesame oil and toss to coat them thoroughly. Set aside to marinate at room temperature for 30 minutes.

Meanwhile, cook the noodles or spaghetti in boiling, salted water until they are just tender. Drain and keep hot.

Heat the remaining oil in a large, deep frying-pan. When it is warm but not hot, add the beef strips and stir-fry for 2 minutes, taking care to keep the strips separate. Push the strips to the side of the pan and add the vegetables. Fry for 1 minute, stirring constantly. Add the sugar, soy sauce and remaining oyster sauce and fry for a further 30 seconds, stirring constantly. Stir the beef strips back into the vegetables the spring onions (scallions) and noodles or spaghetti. Pour over the stock and bring to the boil, stirring constantly. Stir-fry for 2 minutes.

Transfer the mixture to a warmed serving bowl and serve at once.
Serves 4
Preparation and cooking time: $1\frac{1}{4}$ hours

Egg Noodles with Pork Sauce

Metric/Imperial	American
1 large cucumber	1 large cucumber
3 spring onions, finely chopped	3 scallions, finely chopped
4 garlic cloves, crushed	4 garlic cloves, crushed
3 Tbs. vegetable oil	3 Tbs. vegetable oil
$\frac{1}{2}$kg./1lb. lean pork, minced	1lb. lean pork, ground
2 Tbs. rice wine or dry sherry	2 Tbs. rice wine or dry sherry

2 Tbs. Worcestershire sauce	2 Tbs. Worcestershire sauce	Another recipe with an
1 Tbs. soya sauce	1 Tbs. soy sauce	unusual sweet-sour flavour
1 large onion, finely chopped	1 large onion, finely chopped	is Egg Noodles with Pork
2 tsp. brown sugar	2 tsp. brown sugar	Sauce, strongly flavoured
75ml./3fl.oz. chicken stock	⅓ cup chicken stock	with garlic.
350g./12oz. egg noodles	12oz. egg noodles	

Peel the cucumber, then cut in half lengthways. Scoop out the seeds. Cut lengthways into ½cm./¼in. slices, then cut each slice into strips about 5cm./2in. long. Arrange the cucumber and spring onions (scallions) on a serving plate and sprinkle with the garlic. Set aside.

Heat 2 tablespoons of oil in a large frying-pan. When it is hot, add the pork and fry until it loses its pinkness. Stir in the wine or sherry, Worcestershire sauce, soy sauce, onion, sugar and chicken stock, and bring to the boil. Cook for 10 to 15 minutes, or until the liquid has evaporated. Cover the pan and remove from the heat. Keep hot while you cook the noodles.

Cook the noodles in boiling, salted water for 6 to 8 minutes, or until they are just tender. Drain and toss in the remaining oil. Arrange the noodles in a warmed serving dish and cover with the pork sauce. Sprinkle over some of the garnish and serve at once, accompanied by the remaining garnish.

Serves 4-6
Preparation and cooking time: 40 minutes

Transparent Noodles with Beef

Metric/Imperial	American
½kg./1lb. rump of beef, cut across the grain into thin strips	1lb. rump of beef, cut across the grain into thin strips
3 Tbs. soya sauce	3 Tbs. soy sauce
1 Tbs. rice wine or dry sherry	1 Tbs. rice wine or dry sherry
75ml./3fl.oz. peanut oil	⅓ cup peanut oil
2 Tbs. cornflour	2 Tbs. cornstarch
225g./8oz. transparent noodles	8oz. transparent noodles
1½ tsp. sugar	1½ tsp. sugar
1 tsp. salt	1 tsp. salt
175g./6oz. bean sprouts	¾ cup bean sprouts
3 spring onions, finely chopped	3 scallions, finely chopped
50ml./2fl.oz. beef stock	¼ cup beef stock

Put the beef strips into a shallow bowl. Combine 2 tablespoons of soy sauce, the wine or sherry, 1 tablespoon of oil and the cornflour (cornstarch) until they are well blended. Pour the mixture over the beef strips and toss gently to coat them. Set aside to marinate at room temperature for 1 hour.

Meanwhile, put the noodles into a bowl and pour over boiling water. Set aside to soak for 30 minutes. Drain.

Heat the remaining oil in a large frying-pan. When it is hot, add the beef and stir-fry over high heat for 2 minutes. Push the strips to the side of the pan and add the noodles and remaining ingredients. Fry for 1 minute, then stir the beef strips into the noodles. Add the remaining soy sauce and fry for a further 2 minutes, stirring frequently.

Transfer the mixture to a warmed serving dish and serve at once.

Serves 4
Preparation and cooking time: 1¼ hours

Chow Mein

(Fried Noodles)

Metric/Imperial	American
½kg./1lb. egg noodles or spaghetti	1lb. egg noodles or spaghetti
225g./8oz. French beans, chopped	1⅓ cups chopped green beans
50ml./2fl.oz. vegetable oil	¼ cup vegetable oil
1 medium onion, thinly sliced	1 medium onion, thinly sliced
1 garlic clove, crushed	1 garlic clove, crushed
125g./4oz. chicken meat, finely shredded	½ cup finely shredded chicken meat
2 Tbs. soya sauce	2 Tbs. soy sauce
1 tsp. sugar	1 tsp. sugar
1 Tbs. rice wine or dry sherry	1 Tbs. rice wine or dry sherry
20g./¾oz. butter	1½ Tbs. butter
3 Tbs. chicken stock	3 Tbs. chicken stock
½ chicken stock cube, crumbled	½ chicken bouillon cube, crumbled

Cook the noodles or spaghetti in boiling, salted water until they are just tender. Drain the noodles or spaghetti and keep hot. Cook the beans in boiling, salted water for 5 minutes. Drain and keep hot.

Heat the oil in a large frying-pan. When it is hot, add the onion and garlic. Fry for 2 minutes, stirring constantly. Add the chicken and stir-fry for 1 minute. Add the beans, soy sauce, sugar and rice wine or sherry and stir-fry for a further 1½ minutes. Using a slotted spoon, transfer the chicken and bean mixture to a bowl. Keep hot.

Add the butter, stock and stock (bouillon) cube to the oil remaining in the frying-pan. Stir in the noodles or spaghetti and fry for 2 minutes, stirring frequently. Stir in half the bean and chicken mixture, then transfer the whole mixture to a warmed serving dish. Keep hot.

Return the remaining bean and chicken mixture to the pan and increase the heat to high. Stir-fry for 1 minute, adding more oil or soy sauce if necessary. Spoon over the spaghetti mixture and serve at once.

Serves 6
Preparation and cooking time: 40 minutes

Hui Mein

(Noodles in Sauce or Gravy)

Metric/Imperial	American
½kg./1lb. egg noodles or spaghetti	1lb. egg noodles or spaghetti
225g./8oz. French beans, chopped	1⅓ cups chopped green beans
3½ Tbs. vegetable oil	3½ Tbs. vegetable oil
1 large onion, thinly sliced	1 large onion, thinly sliced
1 garlic clove, crushed	1 garlic clove, crushed
2.5cm./1in. piece of fresh root ginger, peeled and chopped	1in. piece of fresh green ginger, peeled and chopped
125g./4oz. chicken meat, finely shredded	½ cup finely shredded chicken meat
3 Tbs. soya sauce	3 Tbs. soy sauce
1 tsp. sugar	1 tsp. sugar
1 Tbs. rice wine or dry sherry	1 Tbs. rice wine or dry sherry
450ml./15fl.oz. chicken stock	2 cups chicken stock
2 tsp. butter	2 tsp. butter
½ chicken stock cube, crumbled	½ chicken bouillon cube, crumbled
1 Tbs. cornflour, mixed to a paste with 4 Tbs. chicken stock	1 Tbs. cornstarch, mixed to a paste with 4 Tbs. chicken stock

Cook the noodles or spaghetti in boiling, salted water until they are just tender. Drain and keep hot. Cook the beans in boiling, salted water for 5 minutes. Drain and keep hot.

Heat the oil in a large frying-pan. When it is hot, add the onion, garlic and ginger. Fry for 1½ minutes, stirring constantly. Add the chicken, beans, 2 tablespoons of soy sauce, the sugar and wine or sherry. Increase the heat to high and stir-fry for 2 minutes. Remove from the heat and keep hot.

Put the stock into a saucepan and bring to the boil. Add the butter, stock (bouillon) cube and the remaining soy sauce and stir well. Add the cornflour (cornstarch) mixture and cook, stirring constantly, until the sauce thickens and becomes translucent. Add the noodles or spaghetti to the saucepan and cook for 2 to 3 minutes, or until they are heated through.

Divide the noodle mixture between four serving bowls. Keep hot.

Return the frying-pan to moderate heat and stir-fry for 1 minute to reheat the bean and chicken mixture. Spoon the mixture over the noodle mixture and serve at once.

Serves 4
Preparation and cooking time: 40 minutes

Two recipes for a sustaining meal with noodles are Tan Mein (on the left) and Cha Chiang Mein (on the right). The former can be eaten not only as a soup but also as a main dish or as a snack, and the latter makes a meal in itself, complete with accompaniments.

27

Tan Mein

(Soup Noodles)

Metric/Imperial	American
350g./12oz. egg noodles or spaghetti	12oz. egg noodles or spaghetti
1½ Tbs. vegetable oil	1½ Tbs. vegetable oil
1 small onion, thinly sliced	1 small onion, thinly sliced
4cm./1½in. piece of fresh root ginger, peeled and chopped	1½in. piece of fresh green ginger, peeled and chopped
225g./8oz. lean pork, finely shredded	8oz. lean pork, finely shredded
15g./½oz. butter	1 Tbs. butter
125g./4oz. mushrooms	1 cup mushrooms
125g./4oz. cabbage, blanched for 1 minute and drained	⅔ cup cabbage, blanched for 1 minute and drained
125g./4oz. bean sprouts, blanched for 1 minute and drained	½ cup bean sprouts, blanched for 1 minute and drained
125g./4oz. shrimps, shelled	⅔ cup peeled shrimp
1½ Tbs. soya sauce	1½ Tbs. soy sauce
1 tsp. sugar	1 tsp. sugar
300ml./10fl.oz. water	1¼ cups water
1 chicken stock cube, crumbled	1 chicken bouillon cube, crumbled
600ml./1 pint chicken or beef stock	2½ cups chicken or beef stock

Cook the noodles or spaghetti in boiling, salted water until they are just tender. Drain and keep hot.

Heat the oil in a large frying-pan. When it is hot, add the onion, ginger and pork and fry for 2 minutes, stirring constantly. Add the butter, and, when it has melted, stir in the mushrooms, cabbage, bean sprouts and shrimps. Stir-fry for 1½ minutes. Stir in the soy sauce and sugar and stir-fry for 1½ minutes. Remove from the heat and keep warm.

Bring the water to the boil in a large saucepan. Reduce the heat to moderate and add the stock (bouillon) cube, stirring until it has dissolved. Add half the pork and fry for 2 minutes, stirring sonstantly. Add the butter and, when it has and simmer for 3 minutes.

Meanwhile, return the frying-pan to high heat and stir-fry the remaining pork mixture for 1 minute.

Divide the noodle mixture between four or six serving bowls. Spoon over the pork mixture and serve at once.

Serves 4-6
Preparation and cooking time: 30 minutes

Cha Chiang Mein

(Noodles in Meat Sauce with Shredded Vegetables)

Traditionally, in this dish, each diner is given a bowl of noodles to which he is expected to add as much meat sauce and shredded vegetables as he likes.

Metric/Imperial	American
½kg./1lb. egg noodles or spaghetti	1lb. egg noodles or spaghetti
3 Tbs. vegetable oil	3 Tbs. vegetable oil
1 medium onion, thinly sliced	1 medium onion, thinly sliced

Metric/Imperial	American
2 garlic cloves, crushed	2 garlic cloves, crushed
4cm./1½in. piece of fresh root ginger, peeled and chopped or ½ tsp. ground ginger	1½in. piece of fresh green ginger, peeled and chopped or ½ tsp. ground ginger
350g./12oz. lean pork or beef, minced	12oz. lean pork or beef, ground
1 Tbs. sesame oil	1 Tbs. sesame oil
5 Tbs. soya sauce	5 Tbs. soy sauce
2 Tbs. rice wine or dry sherry	2 Tbs. rice wine or dry sherry
1 Tbs. sugar	1 Tbs. sugar
1 Tbs. cornflour, mixed to a paste with 4 Tbs. chicken stock	1 Tbs. cornstarch, mixed to a paste with 4 Tbs. chicken stock
SHREDDED VEGETABLES	SHREDDED VEGETABLES
75-125g./3-4oz. (or a heaped side-dishful) shredded cabbage, blanched for 4 minutes and drained	½-⅔ cup (or a heaped side-dishful) shredded cabbage, blanched for 4 minutes and drained
75-125g./3-4oz. (or a heaped side-dishful) shredded carrots, blanched for 4 minutes and drained	½-⅔ cup (or a heaped side-dishful) shredded carrots, blanched for 4 minutes and drained
75-125g./3-4oz. (or a heaped side-dishful) bean sprouts, blanched for 1 minute and drained	⅓-½ cup (or a heaped side-dishful) bean sprouts, blanched for 1 minute and drained
75-125g./3-4oz. (or a heaped side-dishful) shredded cucumber	½-⅔ cup (or a heaped side-dishful) shredded cucumber
50-75g./2-3oz. (or a saucerful) shredded radishes	¼-⅓ cup (or a saucerful) shredded radishes
25-50g./1-2oz. (or a saucerful) mixed pickle	2 Tbs.-¼ cup (or a saucerful) mixed pickle
25-50g./1-2oz. (or a saucerful) chutney	2 Tbs.-¼ cup (or a saucerful) chutney

Arrange the shredded vegetables, pickle and chutney on individual serving dishes and set aside.

Cook the noodles or spaghetti in boiling, salted water until they are just tender. Drain and keep hot.

Heat the oil in a large frying-pan. When it is hot add the onion, garlic and ginger and fry for 1½ minutes, stirring constantly. Add the pork or beef and stir-fry until it loses its pinkness. Stir in the sesame oil, soy sauce, wine or sherry and sugar and stir-fry for a further 3 minutes. Add the cornflour (cornstarch) mixture and cook, stirring constantly, until the sauce thickens and becomes translucent. Remove from the heat and transfer the sauce to a warmed serving bowl.

Divide the noodles or spaghetti between four serving bowls. Serve at once, with the meat sauce and accompaniments.
Serves 4
Preparation and cooking time: 45 minutes

Shrimp Chow Mein

Metric/Imperial	American
vegetable oil for deep-frying	vegetable oil for deep-frying
225g./8oz. thin egg noodles, cooked and drained	8oz. thin egg noodles, cooked and drained
8 dried mushrooms, soaked in cold water for 30 minutes, drained and sliced	8 dried mushrooms, soaked in cold water for 30 minutes, drained and sliced
2 Tbs. peanut oil	2 Tbs. peanut oil
2 carrots, thinly sliced on the diagonal	2 carrots, thinly sliced on the diagonal

An unusual, exotic recipe, Prawn (Shrimp) Chow Mein is usually served on a crisp layer of deep-fried noodles.

225g./8oz. bean sprouts	1 cup bean sprouts
225g./8oz. water chestnuts, sliced	1 cup water chestnuts, sliced
125ml./4fl.oz. chicken stock	½ cup chicken stock
1 Tbs. rice wine or dry sherry	1 Tbs. rice wine or dry sherry
1 Tbs. soya sauce	1 Tbs. soy sauce
350g./12oz. shrimps, shelled	12oz. shrimp, peeled

Fill a large saucepan one-third full with oil and heat until it is very hot. Carefully lower the noodles into the oil and fry for 3 to 4 minutes, or until they are golden brown. Remove from the oil and drain on kitchen towels. Arrange the noodles in a serving dish and keep hot while you prepare the shrimp mixture.

Heat the oil in a large frying-pan. When it is hot, add the mushrooms, carrots, bean sprouts and water chestnuts and fry for 5 minutes, stirring frequently. Pour in the stock and wine or sherry and bring to the boil. Reduce the heat to low and stir in the soy sauce and shrimps. Cover and simmer for 3 to 5 minutes, or until the shrimps are heated through.

Remove from the heat. Make a well in the centre of the noodles and spoon in the shrimp mixture. Serve at once.

Serves 3-4
Preparation and cooking time: 1 hour

Mee Feng Yu Pien

(Sliced Fish in Ground Rice)

Metric/Imperial	American
700g./1½lb. sole fillets, skinned	1½ lb. sole fillets, skinned
4cm./1½in. piece of fresh root ginger, peeled and chopped	1½in. piece of fresh green ginger, peeled and chopped
2 Tbs. soya sauce	2 Tbs. soy sauce
1½ tsp. chilli sauce	1½ tsp. chilli sauce
150g./5oz. coarsely ground rice	1¼ cups coarsely ground rice
SAUCE	SAUCE
2½ Tbs. soya sauce	2½ Tbs. soy sauce
1½ Tbs. tomato purée	1½ Tbs. tomato paste
1 tsp. chilli sauce	1 tsp. chilli sauce
1 Tbs. rice wine or dry sherry	1 Tbs. rice wine or dry sherry
½ Tbs. hoisin sauce	½ Tbs. hoisin sauce
1 Tbs. wine vinegar	1 Tbs. wine vinegar

Cut the sole fillets into thin pieces about 5cm./2in. by 4cm./1½in. Combine the ginger, soy sauce and chilli sauce together and rub the mixture into the sole pieces so that they are evenly coated on both sides. Set aside to marinate for 1 hour.

Heat a large dry frying-pan over moderate heat. Add the rice to the pan and fry, stirring constantly, until it begins to turn brown. Arrange the sole pieces in the pan so that they become thickly coated with the rice. Remove from the heat.

Transfer the sole pieces to a heatproof dish and put the dish into a steamer. Cover and steam over moderate heat for 10 to 12 minutes, or until the fish is cooked through and flakes easily. Remove the dish from the steamer and keep hot.

To make the sauce, combine all the ingredients in a saucepan and cook over moderate heat for 2 minutes, or until it is heated through.

Serve the fish at once, accompanied by the sauce.

Serves 4-6
Preparation and cooking time: 1½ hours

Brown Rice has only the husk removed and, as a result, retains most of its goodness. As it is so nutritious, it is ideal for many vegetarian dishes.

Avorio Rice, a thick, short-grain, absorbent Italian rice, requires slow cooking and is especially suitable for risottos.

Basmati Rice, a long-grain rice, is very popular in Indian cooking. Use as an accompaniment to curries or in rice dishes such as pilaff or biryani.

Rice Paper can be deep-fried and is often used in Chinese cooking as a wrapping for savoury parcels. It is edible.

Wild Rice is technically not a rice, but a water grass grown only in North America. It is expensive but makes an exotic delicacy for special occasions.

Round-Grain Rice is useful in Oriental cooking as it is similar in texture to the rice used in Japanese gohan dishes. It is also suitable for puddings.

Rice Flour, very finely ground rice, is used as an ingredient in baking, such as cakes and biscuits (cookies). It is also an effective thickener.

Ground Rice can be made at home by putting long-grain rice through a grinder. It is a basic ingredient in many sweet and savoury recipes.

Natural Rice is unrefined and is commonly used in wholefood cooking as, through not being milled, it keeps its protein, minerals and vitamins.

1 Brown Rice 2 Avorio Rice 3 Basmati Rice 4 Wild Rice 5 Round-Grain Rice 6 Ground Rice 7 Rice Flour 8 Natural Rice 9 Rice Paper, similar in name only, comes from an Asiatic tree.

33

Pork Fried Rice

Metric/Imperial	American
3 Tbs. vegetable oil	3 Tbs. vegetable oil
1 small onion, thinly sliced	1 small onion, thinly sliced
4cm./1½in. piece of fresh root ginger, peeled and chopped	1½in. piece of fresh green ginger, peeled and chopped
2 celery stalks, thinly sliced on the diagonal	2 celery stalks, thinly sliced on the diagonal
2 small carrots, thinly sliced on the diagonal	2 small carrots, thinly sliced on the diagonal
½ small Chinese or savoy cabbage, shredded	½ small Chinese or savoy cabbage, shredded
225g./8oz. cooked roast pork, cut into strips	1 cup cooked roast pork strips
½ tsp. black pepper	½ tsp. black pepper
2 Tbs. soya sauce	2 Tbs. soy sauce
225g./8oz. cooked long-grain rice	3 cups cooked long-grain rice
2 eggs, lightly beaten	2 eggs, lightly beaten
½ tsp. salt	½ tsp. salt

Heat 2 tablespoons of oil in a large frying-pan. When it is hot, add the onion and ginger. Stir-fry for 2 minutes. Add the celery and carrots and fry for 5 minutes, stirring constantly. Stir in the cabbage, pork, pepper, soy sauce and rice and cook, stirring constantly, for a further 2 to 3 minutes, or until the mixture has heated through. Remove from the heat and keep hot while you make the garnish.

Heat the remaining oil in a small frying-pan. When it is hot, add the beaten eggs and salt and cook for 2 minutes. When the bottom has set, turn the omelet over and cook for a further 2 to 3 minutes, or until it is completely set. Remove from the pan and cut the omelet into strips about 2.5cm /1in. by ½cm./¼in.

Transfer the rice mixture to a warmed serving dish. Garnish with the omelet strips and serve at once.

Serves 4
Preparation and cooking time: 35 minutes

An assortment of vegetables and long-grain rice combine to make Pork Fried Rice a popular and colourful dish.

Chinese Fried Rice

Metric/Imperial	American
225g./8oz. long-grain rice, washed, soaked in cold water for 30 minutes and drained	1⅓ cups long-grain rice, washed, soaked in cold water for 30 minutes and drained
salt	salt
1 Tbs. peanut oil	1 Tbs. peanut oil
2 tsp. soya sauce	2 tsp. soy sauce

Cook the rice in boiling, salted water for 11 minutes, then remove from the heat and drain. Set aside to cool.

Heat the oil in a large frying-pan. When it is hot, add the rice and cook for 1 minute, stirring constantly to coat the rice with the oil. Stir in half the soy sauce and fry, stirring frequently, until the rice is lightly browned. Remove from the heat and stir in the remaining soy sauce. Transfer to a warmed serving dish and serve at once.
Serves 4
Preparation and cooking time: 1½ hours

Chow Fan

(Fried Rice)

Metric/Imperial	American
225g./8oz. long-grain rice, soaked in cold water for 30 minutes and drained	1⅓ cups long-grain rice, soaked in cold water for 30 minutes and drained
450ml./15fl.oz. water	2 cups water
1½ tsp. salt	1½ tsp. salt
2 Tbs. vegetable oil	2 Tbs. vegetable oil
2 medium onions, chopped	2 medium onions, chopped
225g./8oz. cooked ham, finely chopped	1⅔ cups finely chopped cooked ham
2 Tbs. petits pois	2 Tbs. petits pois
2 medium tomatoes, blanched, peeled and quartered	2 medium tomatoes, blanched, peeled and quartered
225g./8oz. frozen shrimps, shelled	1⅓ cups frozen peeled shrimp
1 Tbs. soya sauce	1 Tbs. soy sauce
1 egg, lightly beaten	1 egg, lightly beaten

Put the rice into a saucepan and pour over the water and 1 teaspoon of salt. Bring to the boil, reduce the heat to low and cover the pan. Simmer for 15 to 20 minutes, or until the rice is cooked and tender, and the liquid has been absorbed. Remove from the heat.

Heat the oil in a large saucepan. When it is hot, add the onions and fry, stirring occasionally, until they are soft. Stir in the ham, petits pois, tomatoes, shrimps and remaining salt and cook for 1 minute. Stir in the cooked rice and cook for 2 minutes, stirring constantly. Add the remaining ingredients and stir-fry for 2 minutes.

Transfer the mixture to a warmed serving bowl and serve at once.
Serves 4-6
Preparation and cooking time: 1¼ hours

Chinese omelet, Foo Yung, is often used as a garnish and here it is used as a decoration for Special Fried Rice with Foo Yung.

Special Fried Rice with Foo Yung

Metric/Imperial	American
225g./8oz. long-grain rice, soaked in cold water for 30 minutes and drained	1⅓ cups long-grain rice, soaked in cold water for 30 minutes and drained
600ml./1 pint cold water	2½ cups cold water
1 tsp. salt	1 tsp. salt
5 Tbs. peanut oil	5 Tbs. peanut oil
2 medium onions, finely chopped	2 medium onions, finely chopped
75g./3oz. button mushrooms, sliced	¾ cup sliced button mushrooms

Metric/Imperial	American
4 Tbs. cooked peas	4 Tbs. cooked peas
250g./8oz. peeled shrimps	1⅓ cups peeled shrimp
60g./2oz. cooked ham, shredded	¼ cup shredded cooked ham
FOO YUNG	FOO YUNG
2 large eggs	2 large eggs
1 Tbs. soya sauce	1 Tbs. soy sauce
salt and pepper to taste	salt and pepper to taste
15g./½oz. butter	1 Tbs. butter

Put the rice into a saucepan and pour over the water and salt. Bring to the boil, reduce the heat to low and cover the pan. Simmer for 15 to 20 minutes, or until the rice is cooked and tender and the liquid has been absorbed. Remove from the heat and set aside until cold.

Heat the oil in a large frying-pan. When it is very hot, add the onions, mushrooms, peas and shrimps and stir-fry for 1 minute. Add the ham and stir-fry for 30 seconds. Stir in the cold rice and cook for a further 2 minutes.

Transfer the rice to a warmed ovenproof serving dish and keep warm in the oven while you cook the foo yung.

Beat the eggs, soy sauce and seasoning together until they are frothy. Heat the butter in a 25cm./10in. omelet pan until it stops foaming. Add the egg mixture and stir twice. Leave to set. Preheat the grill (broiler) to moderate.

When the bottom of the foo yung has set, transfer the pan to the grill (broiler) and leave for 1 minute, or until the top is set and browned.

Tip the foo yung on to a plate and cut into strips. Use to decorate the rice mixture and serve at once.

Serves 4-6
Preparation and cooking time: 2 hours

Crab and Ginger Foo Yung

Metric/Imperial	American
6 eggs	6 eggs
3 Tbs. sesame oil	3 Tbs. sesame oil
125g./4oz. crabmeat, shell and cartilage removed and flaked	4 oz. crabmeat, shell and cartilage removed and flaked
4cm./1½in. piece of fresh root ginger, peeled and finely chopped	1½in. piece of fresh green ginger, peeled and finely chopped
2 spring onions, finely chopped	2 scallions, finely chopped
1 Tbs. soya sauce	1 Tbs. soy sauce
1 Tbs. dry sherry	1 Tbs. dry sherry

Beat the eggs until they are frothy. Heat 1 tablespoon of the oil in a small, heavy-based frying-pan. When it is very hot, add the crabmeat, ginger, spring onions (scallions), soy sauce and sherry and stir-fry for 1 minute. Remove the pan from the heat and add the mixture to the eggs. Beat gently to mix.

Put the remaining oil in the frying-pan and return to the heat. When the oil is hot, pour in about a quarter of the egg mixture. Stir with a fork to distribute the mixture and cook for 1 minute. Place a plate over the pan and invert quickly so that the foo yung falls on to the plate. Slide the foo yung back into the pan and cook for a further 1 minute. Turn out in the same way as before and keep warm while you cook the remaining mixture in the same way.

Serves 4
Preparation and cooking time: 20 minutes

Egg Foo Yung

Metric/Imperial	American
4 eggs	4 eggs
1 Tbs. soya sauce	1 Tbs. soy sauce
salt and pepper to taste	salt and pepper to taste
25g./1oz. butter	2 Tbs. butter
1 spring onion, very finely chopped	1 scallion, very finely chopped
125g./4oz. bean sprouts	½ cup bean sprouts

Beat the eggs, soy sauce and seasoning together until the mixture is light and fluffy.

Melt the butter in a frying-pan. Add the spring onion (scallion) and bean sprouts and fry for 4 to 5 minutes, stirring occasionally. Pour in the egg mixture, stir with a fork and leave to set.

Preheat the grill (broiler) to high.

When the bottom of the foo yung has set, transfer the pan to the grill (broiler) and leave for 1 minute or until the top is set and lightly browned.

Serve at once, cut into wedges.

Serves 2-3

Preparation and cooking time: 15 minutes

Shrimp and Egg Foo Yung

Metric/Imperial	American
3 Tbs. vegetable oil	3 Tbs. vegetable oil
225g./8oz. shrimps, chopped	8oz. shelled shrimps, chopped
125g./4oz. mushrooms, sliced	⅔ cup mushrooms, sliced
125g./4oz. bean sprouts	½ cup bean sprouts
4 eggs, lightly beaten	4 eggs, lightly beaten
SAUCE	SAUCE
250ml./8fl.oz. chicken stock	1 cup chicken stock
2 tsp. soy sauce	2 tsp. soy sauce
¼ tsp. salt	¼ tsp. salt
1 Tbs. cornflour, mixed to a paste with 1 Tbs. water	1 Tbs. cornstarch, mixed to a paste with 1 Tbs. water

Heat 1 tablespoon of oil in a frying-pan. When it is hot, add the shrimps and stir-fry for 3 minutes. Remove from the heat and keep hot.

To make the sauce, combine all the ingredients in a small saucepan and bring to the boil, stirring constantly. Cook for 1 minute, stirring constantly, or until the sauce becomes translucent. Set aside.

Combine the mushrooms, bean sprouts, eggs and shrimps and beat together.

Return the frying-pan to the heat and add the remaining oil. When it is hot, add a quarter of the egg mixture and cook for 1 minute, or until the bottom is set and golden brown. Turn the omelet over and cook for a further 1 minute, or until it is just set. Cook the remaining egg mixture in the same way, to make three more omelets.

Return the saucepan to the heat and bring to the boil, stirring constantly. Remove from the heat and pour a little over the omelets. Serve at once, with the sauce.

Serves 4

Preparation and cooking time: 30 minutes

Wonton Dough

Wonton wrappers can be bought from oriental delicatessens, but it isn't very difficult to make your own, using this recipe. Roll out the dough very thinly, to not more than $\frac{1}{8}$cm./$\frac{1}{16}$in. thick, and cut into shapes as you require.

Metric/Imperial	American
450g./1lb. plain flour	4 cups all-purpose flour
2 tsp. salt	2 tsp. salt
2 eggs, lightly beaten with	2 eggs, lightly beaten with
75ml./3fl.oz. water	$\frac{1}{3}$ cup water

Sift the flour and salt into a bowl. Make a well in the centre and pour in the egg mixture. Using your fingers or a spatula, draw the flour into the liquid until it has all been incorporated and the dough comes away from the sides of the bowl.

Turn the dough out on to a lightly floured surface and knead for 10 minutes, or until it is smooth and elastic.

It is now ready to use.

Makes 450g/1 pound (4 cups)
Preparation time: 15 minutes

Shrimp Egg Foo Yung, a more exotic form of the basic Egg Foo Yung, makes an appetizing light meal.

MEAT

Hao Yiu Ngiu Jou Pien

(Quick-fried Beef with Oyster Sauce)

Metric/Imperial	American
700g./1½lb. lean fillet steak, cut into thin strips	1½lb. lean fillet steak, cut into thin strips
1½ tsp. salt	1½ tsp. salt
¼ tsp. white pepper	¼ tsp. white pepper
¼ tsp. ground ginger	¼ tsp. ground ginger
1 Tbs. cornflour	1 Tbs. cornstarch
1 Tbs. soya sauce	1 Tbs. soy sauce
2½ Tbs. oyster sauce	2½ Tbs. oyster sauce
1 tsp. sugar	1 tsp. sugar
2 Tbs. rice wine or dry sherry	2 Tbs. rice wine or dry sherry
75ml./3fl.oz. vegetable oil	⅓ cup vegetable oil
1 medium onion, thinly sliced	1 medium onion, thinly sliced
1 garlic clove, crushed	1 garlic clove, crushed

Rub the beef strips with salt, pepper, ginger and cornflour (cornstarch).

Combine the soy sauce, oyster sauce, sugar and rice wine or sherry in a bowl and set aside.

Heat the oil in a large frying-pan. When it is hot, add the onion and garlic and fry for 30 seconds, stirring constantly. Add the beef to the pan and fry for 2 minutes, stirring constantly. Pour off all but a thin film of oil from the pan.

Pour the reserved oyster sauce mixture over the beef and cook for a further 1½ minutes, stirring constantly. Remove from the heat and transfer the beef slices to a warmed serving dish. Pour over the sauce and serve at once.

Serves 4
Preparation and cooking time: 30 minutes

K'Ou Tse Ngiu Lan

(Leg of Beef in Fruit Sauce)

Metric/Imperial	American
2 Tbs. vegetable oil	2 Tbs. vegetable oil
1 medium onion, thinly sliced	1 medium onion, thinly sliced
2 garlic cloves, crushed	2 garlic cloves, crushed
2.5cm./1in. piece of fresh root ginger, peeled and chopped	1in. piece of fresh green ginger, peeled and chopped
1 x 1½kg./3lb. boned leg of beef, cubed	1 x 3lb. boned leg or shin of beef, cubed
juice of 1 lemon	juice of 1 lemon
juice of 2 oranges	juice of 2 oranges
4 Tbs. soya sauce	4 Tbs. soy sauce
300ml./10fl.oz. red wine	1¼ cups red wine
600ml./1 pint water	2½ cups water
1 tsp. black pepper	1 tsp. black pepper
1 tsp. salt	1 tsp. salt

Preheat the oven to cool 150°C (Gas Mark 2, 300°F).

Heat the oil in a large flameproof casserole. When it is hot, add the onion, garlic and ginger and stir-fry for 1 minute. Add the beef to the casserole and fry for 3 minutes, stirring and turning occasionally. Stir in all the remaining ingredients and bring to the boil, stirring occasionally.

Transfer the casserole to the oven and bake for 4 hours, stirring two or three times during the cooking period. Remove from the oven and serve at once.

Serves 8
Preparation and cooking time: 4½ hours

A side dish of crunchy bean sprouts complements K'Ou Tse Ngiu, a rich, fruity beef stew.

Stir-Fried Beef with Broccoli

Metric/Imperial	American
½kg./1lb. fillet of beef, thinly sliced across the grain into 7.5cm./3in. x 5cm./2in. pieces	1lb. fillet of beef, thinly sliced across the grain into 3in. x 2in. pieces
3 Tbs. soya sauce	3 Tbs. soy sauce
1 Tbs. rice wine or dry sherry	1 Tbs. rice wine or dry sherry
2.5cm./1in. piece of fresh root ginger, peeled and chopped	1in. piece of fresh green ginger, peeled and chopped
50ml./2fl.oz. vegetable oil	¼ cup vegetable oil
½kg./1lb. broccoli, broken into flowerets	1lb. broccoli, broken into flowerets
75ml./3fl.oz. beef stock	⅓ cup beef stock
15g./½oz. vegetable fat	1 Tbs. vegetable fat
2 tsp. cornflour, mixed to a paste with 4 Tbs. water	2 tsp. cornstarch, mixed to a paste with 4 Tbs. water

Put the beef strips in a shallow bowl. Combine the soy sauce, wine or sherry, ginger and 1 tablespoon of oil together, then pour over the strips, basting to coat them thoroughly. Set aside to marinate at room temperature for 10 minutes, stirring occasionally. Meanwhile, cut the broccoli into bite-sized pieces.

Heat the remaining oil in a large frying-pan. When it is hot, add the beef mixture and stir-fry for 1½ minutes. Using a slotted spoon, transfer the beef strips to a plate. Add the beef stock to the pan and bring to the boil, stirring constantly. Add the broccoli and fry for 1 minute, stirring constantly. Reduce the heat to very low, cover and simmer the mixture for 4 minutes. Using the slotted spoon, transfer the broccoli to a warmed serving dish. Keep hot while you finish off the meat.

Add the vegetable fat to the pan and melt it. Return the beef strips to the pan and stir-fry for 30 seconds. Add the cornflour (cornstarch) and stir-fry for 1 minute, or until the sauce becomes translucent. Remove from the heat.

Using the slotted spoon, transfer the beef strips over the broccoli, then pour over the sauce. Serve at once.

Serves 4
Preparation and cooking time: 35 minutes

Gingered Beef

Metric/Imperial	American
2 tsp. ground ginger	2 tsp. ground ginger
5 Tbs. soya sauce	5 Tbs. soy sauce
2 tsp. cornflour	2 tsp. cornstarch
½ tsp. sugar	½ tsp. sugar
700g./1½lb. rump steak, thinly sliced across the grain	1½lb. rump steak, thinly sliced across the grain
50ml./2fl.oz. vegetable oil	¼ cup vegetable oil
5cm./2in. piece of fresh root ginger, peeled and chopped	2in. piece of fresh green ginger, peeled and chopped
125g./4oz. bamboo shoots, cubed	½ cup cubed bamboo shoots
4 dried mushrooms, soaked in cold water for 30 minutes, drained and sliced	4 dried mushrooms, soaked in cold water for 30 minutes, drained and sliced

Combine the ground ginger, soy sauce, cornflour (cornstarch) and sugar together until they are well blended. Stir in the meat slices and baste them thoroughly. Set aside to marinate at room temperature for 1 hour, basting occasionally. Remove the meat from the marinade and pat dry with kitchen towels. Discard the marinade.

Heat the oil in a large frying-pan. When it is hot, add the ginger and fry for 3 minutes, stirring constantly. Stir in the meat, bamboo shoots and mushrooms and fry, stirring and turning occasionally, for 6 to 8 minutes, or until the meat is cooked through.

Transfer the mixture to a warmed serving dish and serve at once.

Serves 4-6
Preparation and cooking time: 1¾ hours

A quick and easy dish to make, Stir-Fried Beef with Broccoli, served with Fried Rice, is filling and tasty.

Quick Fried Beef with 'Triple Shreds'

Quick Fried Beef with 'Triple Shreds' is ideal for practising the Chinese method of eating with chopsticks.

Metric/Imperial	American
½kg./1lb. fillet of beef, sliced across the grain, then cut into strips	1lb. fillet of beef, sliced across the grain, then cut into strips
3 Tbs. soya sauce	3 Tbs. soy sauce
1 Tbs. dry sherry	1 Tbs. dry sherry
1 tsp. sugar	1 tsp. sugar
salt and pepper to taste	salt and pepper to taste
3 Tbs. vegetable oil	3 Tbs. vegetable oil
2.5cm./1in. piece of fresh root ginger, peeled and thinly sliced	1in. piece of fresh green ginger, peeled and thinly sliced
1 large leek, white part only, sliced	1 large leek, white part only, sliced

1 onion, thinly sliced

25g./1oz. butter

1 onion, thinly sliced

2 Tbs. butter

Put the beef strips in a shallow bowl. Combine the soy sauce, sherry, sugar and salt and pepper and pour over the strips, rubbing the mixture into the meat with your fingers. Set aside for 10 minutes.

Heat the oil in a frying-pan. When the oil is very hot, add the ginger, leek and onion and stir-fry for 1 minute over moderately high heat.

Transfer to a warmed plate and set aside.

Add the butter to the pan and melt it over moderately high heat. Add the beef strips and stir-fry for 1 minute. Return the vegetables to the pan and stir-fry for a further 1 minute.

Transfer the mixture to a warmed dish and serve.

Serves 4

Preparation and cooking time: 20 minutes

Braised Beef in Soy Sauce

Metric/Imperial	American
300ml./10fl.oz. water	1¼ cups water
3 Tbs. soya sauce	3 Tbs. soy sauce
5 Tbs. rice wine or dry sherry	5 Tbs. rice wine or dry sherry
1 Tbs. sugar	1 Tbs. sugar
1 Tbs. salt	1 Tbs. salt
3 Tbs. vegetable oil	3 Tbs. vegetable oil
1kg./2lb. braising steak, cubed	2lb. chuck steak, cubed

Combine the water, soy sauce, wine or sherry, sugar and salt and set aside.

Heat half the oil in a large frying-pan for 30 seconds. Add half the meat to the pan and fry for 2 minutes, stirring and turning constantly. Transfer the cubes to a plate. Add the remaining oil and remaining beef cubes to the pan and fry until they are lightly browned. Return the first batch of cubes to the pan and stir in the soy sauce mixture. Bring to the boil. Cover, reduce the heat to low and simmer for 1½ to 2 hours, stirring occasionally, or until the beef is cooked through and tender.

Transfer the mixture to a warmed serving dish and serve at once.

Serves 6
Preparation and cooking time: 2¼ hours

Hung Shao Ngiu Jou

(Red-Cooked Beef with Star Anise)

Metric/Imperial	American
75ml./3fl.oz. vegetable oil	⅓ cup vegetable oil
1 x 1½-2kg./3-4lb. leg or shin of beef, cubed	1 x 3-4lb. leg or shin of beef, cubed
3 pieces star anise	3 pieces star anise
150ml./5fl.oz. water	⅔ cup water
½ beef stock cube, crumbled	½ beef bouillon cube, crumbled
7 Tbs. soya sauce	7 Tbs. soy sauce
2.5cm./1in. piece of fresh root ginger, peeled and finely chopped	1in. piece of fresh green ginger, peeled and finely chopped
2 tsp. sugar	2 tsp. sugar
150ml./5fl.oz. red wine	⅔ cup red wine

Preheat the oven to cool 150°C (Gas Mark 2, 300°F).

Heat the oil in a flameproof casserole. When it is hot, add the beef cubes and fry until they are evenly browned. Remove from the heat and pour off all the excess oil.

Stir in the star anise, water, stock (bouillon) cube and 4 tablespoons of soy sauce. Return the casserole to the heat and bring to the boil, stirring constantly. Transfer to the oven and cook for 1 hour, turning the meat once.

Remove from the oven and stir in the remaining ingredients. Return to the oven and cook for a further 2 hours, turning the meat every 30 minutes.

Remove from the oven and serve at once.

Serves 8-10
Preparation and cooking time: 3½ hours

Stir-Fried Beef with Mixed Vegetables and Peanuts

Metric/Imperial	American
½kg./1lb. rump steak, thinly sliced across the grain, then cut into strips	1lb. rump steak, thinly sliced across the grain, then cut into strips
salt and pepper to taste	salt and pepper to taste
1 tsp. ground ginger	1 tsp. ground ginger
1 Tbs. cornflour	1 Tbs. cornstarch
50ml./2fl.oz. peanut oil	¼ cup peanut oil
5cm./2in. piece of fresh root ginger, peeled and chopped	2in. piece of fresh green ginger, peeled and chopped
175g./6oz. bean sprouts	¾ cup bean sprouts
2 spring onions, chopped	2 scallions, chopped
3 Tbs. unsalted peanuts	3 Tbs. unsalted peanuts
2 Tbs. soya sauce	2 Tbs. soy sauce
1 tsp. wine vinegar	1 tsp. wine vinegar
1 tsp. brown sugar	1 tsp. brown sugar

Rub the beef strips with the salt, pepper, ginger and cornflour (cornstarch).

Heat the oil in a large, deep frying-pan. When it is hot, add the root (green) ginger and fry for 1 minute, stirring constantly.

Add the beef and stir-fry for 2 minutes. Stir in the vegetables and peanuts and fry for 2 minutes, stirring constantly. Add the remaining ingredients and stir-fry for a further 1½ minutes.

Transfer the mixture to a warmed serving dish and serve at once.

Serves 4
Preparation and cooking time: 30 minutes

Sweet and Sour Beef

Metric/Imperial	American
2 Tbs. cornflour	2 Tbs. cornstarch
1 Tbs. soya sauce	1 Tbs. soy sauce
300ml./10fl.oz. beef stock	1¼ cups beef stock
2 Tbs. tomato purée	2 Tbs. tomato paste
2 Tbs. red wine vinegar	2 Tbs. red wine vinegar
2 tsp. clear honey	2 tsp. clear honey
4 Tbs. peanut oil	4 Tbs. peanut oil
2 large red peppers, pith and seeds removed and cut into small pieces	2 large red peppers, pith and seeds removed and cut into small pieces
1 large onion, finely chopped	1 large onion, finely chopped
1 garlic clove, crushed	1 garlic clove, crushed
4cm./1½in. piece of fresh root ginger, peeled and finely chopped	1½in. piece of fresh green ginger, peeled and finely chopped
700g./1½lb. rump of beef, cut into 5cm./2in. slivers	1½lb. rump of beef, cut into 2in. slivers

Accompanied by Chinese Fried Rice and Chinese Roast Pork, Ching-chiao-ch'ao niu jou is a delicious mixture of rump steak and beansprouts, tomatoes and green peppers.

Combine the cornflour (cornstarch), soy sauce, beef stock, tomato purée (paste), vinegar and honey in a small bowl, beating until they are well blended. Set aside.

Heat half the oil in a large frying-pan. When it is very hot, add the red peppers, onion, garlic and ginger and stir-fry for 2 minutes. Using a slotted spoon, transfer the vegetable mixture to a plate.

Add the remaining oil to the frying-pan. When it is very hot, add the beef strips and stir-fry for 3 minutes, or until they are evenly browned.

Stir in the reserved peppers, onion, ginger and garlic mixture until it is thoroughly blended.

Pour the cornflour (cornstarch) and stock mixture into the pan and bring to the boil, stirring constantly. Cook the mixture over moderate heat until the sauce thickens and becomes translucent.

Transfer the mixture to a warmed serving dish and serve at once.

Serves 4-6
Preparation and cooking time: 25 minutes

Ching-Chiao-Chao Niu Jou

(Steak with Pepper)

Metric/Imperial	American
½kg./1lb. rump steak, cut 2.5cm./1in. thick	1lb. rump steak, cut 1in. thick
4 Tbs. peanut oil	4 Tbs. peanut oil
2 garlic cloves, crushed	2 garlic cloves, crushed
salt and pepper	salt and pepper
4 Tbs. soya sauce	4 Tbs. soy sauce
2 tsp. sugar	2 tsp. sugar
225g./8oz. bean sprouts	1 cup bean sprouts
2 tomatoes, blanched, peeled and quartered	2 tomatoes, blanched, peeled and quartered
2 green peppers, pith and seeds removed, and coarsely diced	2 green peppers, pith and seeds removed, and coarsely diced
½ Tbs. cornflour, mixed to a paste with 2 Tbs. cold water	½ Tbs. cornstarch mixed to a paste with 2 Tbs. cold water
4 spring onions, sliced	4 scallions, sliced

Cut the beef diagonally into short, thin strips.

Heat the oil in a heavy frying-pan. When it is hot, mix in the garlic and salt and pepper to taste. Add the beef and stir-fry for 3 to 4 minutes or until it is golden brown.

Increase the heat to high. Stir in the soy sauce and sugar, cover and cook for 5 minutes.

Uncover and stir in the bean sprouts, tomatoes and peppers. Re-cover and cook for 5 minutes.

Stir in the cornflour (cornstarch) mixture until the mixture thickens and becomes translucent.

Transfer to a warmed serving dish and sprinkle over the spring onions (scallions).

Serves 4
Preparation and cooking time: 25 minutes

Sweet and Sour Liver

Metric/Imperial	American
700g./1½lb. lambs' liver, cut into 7.5cm./3in. by 5cm./2in. pieces	1½lb. lambs' liver, cut into 3in. by 2in. pieces
vegetable oil for deep-frying	vegetable oil for deep-frying
MARINADE	MARINADE
5 Tbs. soya sauce	5 Tbs. soy sauce
2 Tbs. rice wine or dry sherry	2 Tbs. rice wine or dry sherry
2 tsp. sugar	2 tsp. sugar
SAUCE	SAUCE
4 Tbs. wine vinegar	4 Tbs. wine vinegar
3 Tbs. sugar	3 Tbs. sugar
3 Tbs. orange juice	3 Tbs. orange juice
1 Tbs. tomato purée	1 Tbs. tomato paste
1½ Tbs. soya sauce	1½ Tbs. soy sauce
1½ Tbs. rice wine or dry sherry	1½ Tbs. rice wine or dry sherry
1 Tbs. cornflour, mixed to a paste with 5 Tbs. water	1 Tbs. cornstarch, mixed to a paste with 5 Tbs. water

Combine all the marinade ingredients in a large bowl and add the liver pieces. Baste well, then set aside at room temperature for 3 hours, basting occasionally. Remove the liver from the marinade and pat dry with kitchen towels. Discard the marinade.

Fill a large saucepan one-third full with oil and heat until it is very hot. Carefully lower the liver strips into the oil, a few at a time, and fry for 1 minute, or until they are browned and crisp. Remove the liver from the oil and drain on kitchen towels.

Combine all the sauce ingredients in a saucepan and bring to the boil, stirring constantly. Add the liver pieces to the sauce and cook, stirring constantly, until the sauce thickens and becomes translucent. Remove from the heat and transfer the mixture to a warmed serving dish. Serve at once.

Serves 4
Preparation and cooking time: 3½ hours

Run Tsa Chin Kan

(Plain Deep-Fried Liver and Kidneys)

Metric/Imperial	American
350g./12oz. lambs' liver	12oz. lambs' liver
350g./12oz. lambs' kidneys, trimmed	12oz. lambs' kidneys, trimmed
5 Tbs. soya sauce	5 Tbs. soy sauce
2 Tbs. rice wine or dry sherry	2 Tbs. rice wine or dry sherry
2 tsp. sugar	2 tsp. sugar
vegetable oil for deep-frying	vegetable oil for deep-frying
DIP	DIP
1 Tbs. black pepper	1 Tbs. black pepper
1 Tbs. salt	1 Tbs. salt

Slice the liver and kidneys thinly then cut the slices into uniform strips, about 4cm./1½in. by 2.5cm./1in. Put the liver strips in one bowl and the kidney strips in another.

Combine the soy sauce, wine or sherry and sugar until they are well blended. Pour equal amounts over the liver and kidneys and toss gently until the strips are thoroughly coated. Set aside to marinate at room temperature for 3 hours, basting occasionally.

Fill a large saucepan one-third full with oil and heat until it is hot. Carefully lower the liver strips into the oil and fry for 1 minute, or until they are browned and crisp. Remove from the oil and drain on kitchen towels. Keep hot while you fry the kidney strips in the same way.

To make the dip, fry the salt and pepper in a small frying-pan over moderately low heat for 4 minutes, stirring constantly. Remove from the heat and transfer the mixture to a small bowl. Serve the liver and kidney strips at once, with the dip.

Serves 4
Preparation and cooking time: 3½ hours

Marinated and deep-fried, Run Tsa Chin Kan is an unusual recipe for succulent liver and kidneys.

Shao k'o Yang Jou

(Steamed Lamb)

Metric/Imperial	American
1 x 1½kg./3lb. leg of lamb	1 x 3lb. leg of lamb
1 tsp. crushed black peppercorns	1 tsp. crushed black peppercorns
5cm./2in. piece of fresh root ginger, peeled and finely chopped or grated	2in. piece of fresh green ginger, peeled and finely chopped or grated
125g./4oz. mixed sweet pickle	½ cup mixed sweet pickle
75ml./3fl.oz. soya sauce	⅓ cup soy sauce
150ml./5fl.oz. dry sherry	⅔ cup dry sherry
2 onions, thinly sliced	2 onions, thinly sliced
1 tsp. butter	1 tsp. butter

Half-fill a saucepan with water and bring to the boil. Add the lamb, cover and boil for 4 minutes over moderately high heat.

Remove the pan from the heat and drain the lamb. Put the lamb on a chopping board and cut it, including the skin, into cubes. Arrange the cubes, skin side down, on the bottom of a heatproof basin. Sprinkle over the peppercorns and ginger and spoon over the pickle.

Combine the soy sauce and sherry and pour over the lamb. Arrange the onions on top. Cover tightly with a greased circle of greaseproof or waxed paper and foil about 10cm./4in. wider than the rim of the basin and tie with string.

Put the basin in a large saucepan and pour in enough boiling water to come about two-thirds of the way up the basin. Cover and place over low heat. Steam for 2½ hours, adding more boiling water if necessary.

When the lamb has finished steaming, lift the basin out of the water and remove the paper and foil circles. Transfer the mixture to a warmed dish and serve.

Serves 6
Preparation and cooking time: 2¾ hours

Crispy Roast Pork

Metric/Imperial	American
1 x 1½kg./3lb. belly of pork	1 x 3lb. belly or bacon of pork
1½ Tbs. salt	1½ Tbs. salt
1 tsp. 5-spice powder	1 tsp. 5-spice powder
1½ Tbs. cornflour, mixed to a paste with 1 egg white	1½ Tbs. cornstarch, mixed to a paste with 1 egg white
SAUCE	SAUCE
4 Tbs. soya sauce	4 Tbs. soy sauce
4 Tbs. tomato ketchup	4 Tbs. tomato ketchup

Rub the pork all over with the salt and spice powder. Set aside at room temperature for 8 hours or overnight.

Preheat the oven to fairly hot 190°C (Gas Mark 5, 375°F).

Quickly dip the pork in a saucepan half-filled with boiling water—the meat should be in the water for only a second or two. Dry with kitchen towels, then rub all over with the cornflour (cornstarch) mixture.

Place the pork on a rack in a roasting pan and put in the oven. Roast for 1¼ hours, or until it is completely cooked through.

Transfer the pork to a carving board and cut, through the skin, into $\frac{1}{2}$cm./$\frac{1}{4}$in. thick slices (each one should have a little skin attached to it).

Combine the soy sauce and ketchup, then serve with the pork.

Serves 4
Preparation and cooking time: 9$\frac{1}{2}$ hours

Crispy Roast Pork (left) has a crunchy outer layer and juicy tender centre. Steamed Lamb (right) is succulent and spicy.

53

Jou Si Chow Ching Ts'Ai

(Shredded Pork Stir-fried with Spring Greens)

Metric/Imperial	American
350g./12oz. lean pork, cut into strips	12oz. lean pork, cut into thin strips
½ tsp. salt	½ tsp. salt
¼ tsp. black pepper	¼ tsp. black pepper
2 tsp. cornflour	2 tsp. cornstarch
3 Tbs. vegetable oil	3 Tbs. vegetable oil
½kg./1lb. spring greens or cabbage, shredded	2½ cups shredded collards or cabbage
15g./½oz. vegetable fat	1 Tbs. vegetable fat
50ml./2fl.oz. beef stock	¼ cup beef stock
2 Tbs. soya sauce	2 Tbs. soy sauce
1 tsp. sugar	1 tsp. sugar
2 Tbs. dry sherry	2 Tbs. dry sherry

Put the pork strips on a plate and sprinkle them with the salt, pepper and corn-flour (cornstarch), rubbing them into the flesh with your fingers.

Heat the oil in a large frying-pan. When it is hot, add the pork and fry for 3 minutes, stirring constantly. Push the pork strips to the side of the pan and add the greens (collards) or cabbage with the vegetable fat. Stir and mix the greens (collards) or cabbage with the remainder of the oil and the vegetable fat. Reduce the heat to moderate and stir in the stock, soy sauce and sugar. Fry the greens (collards) or cabbage for 3 minutes, turning constantly.

Stir the pork strips into the vegetables. Pour over the wine or sherry and fry for a further 1 minute, stirring constantly. Remove from the heat and transfer to a warmed serving dish. Serve at once.

Serves 4
Preparation and cooking time: 30 minutes

Cantonese Roast Pork

Metric/Imperial	American
1 x 1½kg./3lb. loin of pork, trimmed	1 x 3lb. loin of pork, trimmed
50ml./2fl.oz. soya sauce	¼ cup soy sauce
4 Tbs. soft brown sugar	4 Tbs. soft brown sugar
½ tsp. 5-spice powder	½ tsp. 5-spice powder
2 Tbs. dry sherry	2 Tbs. dry sherry
4cm./1½in. piece of fresh root ginger, peeled and sliced	1½in. piece of fresh green ginger, peeled and sliced

Cut the meat in half. Mix the soy sauce, sugar, five-spice powder, sherry and ginger together in a large shallow dish. Put in the pork and set aside to marinate at room temperature for 4 hours, basting frequently.

Preheat the oven to fairly hot 190°C (Gas Mark 5, 375°F). Put the pork and marinade in a roasting pan and roast for 10 minutes. Turn the meat over and increase the temperature to very hot 230°C (Gas Mark 8, 450°F). Continue to roast for about 40 minutes, turning and basting frequently during cooking. Test the meat for doneness with a skewer; the juice should run out clear.

Preheat the grill (broiler) to high.

Put the meat under the grill (broiler), and grill (broil) for 4 to 6 minutes, or until it is evenly browned.

Transfer to a serving dish, discarding the marinade, and slice before serving.

Serves 6
Preparation and cooking time: 5¼ hours

Yu Hsiang Jou si

(Quick-Fried Shredded Pork with 'Fish' Ingredients)

This dish comes from the province of Szechuan in Western China, where there is a tradition of cooking spicy dishes.

Metric/Imperial	American
½kg./1lb. pork fillet, thinly sliced and shredded	1lb. pork tenderloin, thinly sliced and shredded
4 Tbs. soya sauce	4 Tbs. soy sauce
2 tsp. cornflour, mixed to a paste with 2 Tbs. water	2 tsp. cornstarch, mixed to a paste with 2 Tbs. water
5 Tbs. vegetable oil	5 Tbs. vegetable oil
2 Tbs. fried salted black beans, soaked in cold water for 15 minutes, drained and chopped	2 Tbs. fried salted black beans, soaked in cold water for 15 minutes, drained and chopped
2 small dried chillis, finely chopped	2 small dried chillis, finely chopped
2 garlic cloves, crushed	2 garlic cloves, crushed
4 dried mushrooms, soaked in cold water for 30 minutes, drained and finely chopped	4 dried mushrooms, soaked in cold water for 30 minutes, drained and finely chopped
1 leek, white part only, finely chopped	1 leek, white part only, finely chopped
1 Tbs. 'wood ear' fungi	1 Tbs. 'wood ear' fungi
2.5cm./1in. piece of fresh root ginger, peeled and finely chopped	1in. piece of fresh green ginger, peeled and finely chopped
75g./3oz. bamboo shoots, finely chopped	⅓ cup finely chopped bamboo shoots
2 tsp. sesame oil	2 tsp. sesame oil
1½ Tbs. wine vinegar	1½ Tbs. wine vinegar
2 Tbs. dry sherry	2 Tbs. dry sherry
1½ tsp. sugar	1½ tsp. sugar

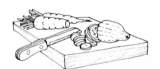

Combine the pork and 2 tablespoons of soy sauce. Work the sauce into the meat with your fingers. Add the cornflour (cornstarch) mixture and stir to blend. Set aside for 10 minutes.

Heat 3 tablespoons of oil in a deep frying-pan. When it is hot, add the pork mixture, spreading it out over the bottom of the pan. Stir-fry for 1 minute. Transfer the pork to a plate.

Add the remaining oil to the pan. When it is hot, add the black beans and chillis and stir-fry for 10 seconds. Increase the heat to moderately high and add the garlic, mushrooms, leek, 'wood ear' fungi, ginger and bamboo shoots. Stir-fry for 3 minutes. Return the pork to the pan and stir in the sesame oil, remaining soy sauce, vinegar, sherry and sugar. Stir-fry for 1½ minutes, or until the mixture is heated through.

Transfer to a warmed dish and serve.

Serves 4
Preparation and cooking time: 30 minutes

Lou Jou

(Pork Simmered in Master Sauce)

Metric/Imperial	American
1 x 1½kg./3lb. leg of pork, boned and trimmed of excess fat	1 x 3lb. leg of pork, boned and trimmed of excess fat
SAUCE	SAUCE
600ml./1 pint soya sauce	2½ cups soy sauce
300ml./10fl.oz. rice wine or dry sherry	1¼ cups rice wine or dry sherry
150ml./5fl.oz. chicken stock	⅔ cup chicken stock
4 Tbs. soft brown sugar	4 Tbs. soft brown sugar
2 garlic cloves, crushed	2 garlic cloves, crushed
2.5cm./1in. piece of fresh root ginger, peeled and chopped	1in. piece of fresh green ginger, peeled and chopped
2 bouquets garnis	2 bouquets garnis

Put the pork in a large saucepan and just cover with water. Bring to the boil, reduce the heat to moderate and cook for 6 minutes. Remove from the heat, drain the pork and set aside. Discard the cooking liquid.

To prepare the sauce, combine all the ingredients together until they are thoroughly blended. Bring to the boil, stirring frequently. Reduce the heat to low and carefully arrange the pork in the sauce, immersing it completely. Simmer for 1½ hours, turning the pork every 30 minutes.

Remove from the heat and transfer the pork to a carving board. Cut the meat into thin slices and arrange the slices decoratively on a warmed serving dish. Strain the sauce into a sauceboat and pour a little over and around the meat. Serve at once, accompanied by the remaining sauce.

Serves 6
Preparation and cooking time: 2 hours

All the main ingredients must be shredded into very fine strips so essential to the texture of this well-flavoured dish of Pork with Bamboo Shoots.

Pork with Bamboo Shoots

Metric/Imperial	American
700g./1½lb. pork fillet, cut across the grain into thin strips	1½lb. pork tenderloin, cut across the grain into thin strips
75ml./3fl.oz. soya sauce	⅓ cup soy sauce
1 Tbs. rice wine or dry sherry	1 Tbs. rice wine or dry sherry
2 tsp. cornflour	2 tsp. cornstarch
150ml./5fl.oz. groundnut or peanut oil	⅔ cup groundnut or peanut oil
1 leek, thinly sliced crosswise on the diagonal	1 leek, thinly sliced crosswise on the diagonal
450g./1lb. bamboo shoots, thinly sliced on the diagonal	1lb. bamboo shoots, thinly sliced on the diagonal
2 tsp. sugar	2 tsp. sugar

Put the pork strips in a bowl. Combine 2 tablespoons of soy sauce, the rice wine or sherry and cornflour (cornstarch) until they are well blended, and pour over the pork. Toss the strips gently to coat them thoroughly. Set aside to marinate for 10 minutes, basting occasionally.

Heat a large frying-pan over high heat for 30 seconds. Add the oil and swirl it around the pan. Add the pork and leek and fry for 5 minutes, stirring constantly. Stir in the bamboo shoots. Stir in the remaining soy sauce and sugar, reduce the heat to low and simmer the mixture for 10 minutes, stirring frequently.

Transfer the mixture to a warmed serving bowl and serve at once.
Serves 4
Preparation and cooking time: 45 minutes

Hung Shao Chu Jo

(Red-Cooked Pork in Soy Sauce)

Metric/Imperial	American
1 x 2kg./4lb. belly of pork	1 x 4lb. belly or bacon of pork
75ml./3fl.oz. vegetable oil	⅓ cup vegetable oil
7 Tbs. soya sauce	7 Tbs. soy sauce
1 Tbs. sugar	1 Tbs. sugar
150ml./5fl.oz. chicken or beef stock	⅔ cup chicken or beef stock
150ml./5fl.oz. red wine	⅔ cup red wine

Preheat the oven to warm 170°C (Gas Mark 3, 325°F).

Cut the pork through the skin into 12 pieces. Heat the oil in a flameproof casserole. When it is hot, add the pork slices and fry until they are evenly browned. Remove from the heat and pour off excess oil. Add 4 tablespoons of the soy sauce, half the sugar and 75ml./3fl.oz. (⅓ cup) each of the stock and wine. Turn the meat in this sauce several times. Return to the heat and bring to the boil.

Transfer the casserole to the oven and roast for 1 hour, turning the meat once. Remove from the oven and add the remaining soy sauce, sugar, stock and wine. Turn the meat over several times. Return the casserole to the oven and reduce the oven temperature to cool 150°C (Gas Mark 2, 300°F). Roast for a further 1 hour, turning the meat once.

Remove from the oven and serve at once.
Serves 4-6
Preparation and cooking time: 2½ hours

Colourful Pork Balls with Ginger is served here with refreshing jasmine tea.

Shao Jou 1

(Cantonese Roast Pork)

Metric/Imperial	American
1½kg./3lb. pork fillets, cut into strips about 15cm./6in. long by 4cm./1½in. thick	3lb. pork tenderloin, cut into strips about 6in. long by 1½in. thick
2 Tbs. vegetable oil	2 Tbs. vegetable oil
MARINADE	MARINADE
1 onion, very finely chopped	1 onion, very finely chopped
5 Tbs. soya sauce	5 Tbs. soy sauce
1 Tbs. sugar	1 Tbs. sugar
1 Tbs. dry sherry	1 Tbs. dry sherry
1½ tsp. ground ginger	1½ tsp. ground ginger
1 Tbs. hoisin sauce (optional)	1 Tbs. hoisin sauce (optional)

To make the marinade, combine all the ingredients and beat well. Add the pork strips and baste to coat. Set aside at room temperature for 2 hours, basting occasionally.

Preheat the oven to moderate 180°C (Gas Mark 4, 350°F).

Remove the pork from the marinade and reserve the marinade. Put the strips in a roasting pan, large enough to take them in one layer, then baste with half the marinade and 1 tablespoon of oil. Put the pan into the oven and roast for 15 minutes. Remove from the oven and turn over the strips. Baste again with the marinade and remaining oil and return the pan to the oven. Roast the pork for a further 15 minutes.

Transfer the pork to a chopping board and cut the strips into thin slices before serving.

Serves 6-8
Preparation and cooking time: 2¾ hours

Pork Balls with Ginger

Metric/Imperial	American
700g./1½lb. minced pork	1½lb. ground pork
2.5cm./1in. piece of fresh root ginger, peeled and finely chopped	1in. piece of fresh green ginger, peeled and finely chopped
4 water chestnuts, drained and finely chopped	4 water chestnuts, drained and finely chopped
1 egg	1 egg
1 tsp. salt	1 tsp. salt
1 Tbs. soya sauce	1 Tbs. soy sauce
5 Tbs. cornflour	5 Tbs. cornstarch
1 tsp. sugar	1 tsp. sugar
8 dried mushrooms, soaked in cold water for 30 minutes	8 dried mushrooms, soaked in cold water for 30 minutes
1 bamboo shoot	1 bamboo shoot
1 red pepper, pith and seeds removed	1 red pepper, pith and seeds removed
1 green pepper, pith and seeds removed	1 green pepper, pith and seeds removed
8 Tbs. vegetable oil	8 Tbs. vegetable oil
SAUCE	SAUCE
5 Tbs. wine vinegar	5 Tbs. wine vinegar
5 Tbs. dry sherry	5 Tbs. dry sherry
2 Tbs. sugar	2 Tbs. sugar
2 Tbs. tomato purée	2 Tbs. tomato paste
salt and pepper to taste	salt and pepper to taste
1 tsp. cornflour, mixed to a paste with 2 Tbs. water	1 tsp. cornstarch, mixed to a paste with 2 Tbs. water

Combine the pork, ginger, water chestnuts, egg, salt, soy sauce, 2 tablespoons of cornflour (cornstarch) and sugar thoroughly. Shape into walnut-sized balls. Put the remaining cornflour (cornstarch) on a plate and roll the balls in it to coat them.

Remove the mushrooms from the water and squeeze dry. Remove and discard the stalks. Cut them, and the other vegetables, into equal-sized dice.

Heat 6 tablespoons of the oil in a frying-pan. When it is hot, reduce the heat to moderately low and add the pork balls. Fry, turning frequently, for 15 minutes or until they are cooked through and crisp. Transfer to a warmed dish. Cover and keep hot.

Combine all the sauce ingredients together, except the cornflour (cornstarch).

Pour off and discard the oil in the pan. Rinse and wipe the pan dry, and return it to high heat for 30 seconds. Add the remaining oil and reduce the heat to moderate. Heat for a further 30 seconds. Add the vegetables and stir-fry for 3 minutes. Pour over the sauce and stir-fry for a further 3 minutes. Stir in the cornflour (cornstarch) mixture and stir-fry until the sauce becomes translucent and thickens. Pour over the pork balls and serve.

Serves 4
Preparation and cooking time: 50 minutes

Shih-Tzu-Tou, pork balls served on a layer of Chinese cabbage, is a traditional dish.

Shih-Tzu-Tou

(Pork and Cabbage Casserole)

Metric/Imperial	American
½kg./1lb. lean pork, minced	1lb. lean pork, ground
1 shallot, finely chopped	1 shallot, finely chopped
4 water chestnuts, chopped	4 water chestnuts, chopped
2.5cm./1in. piece of fresh root ginger, peeled and chopped	1in. piece of fresh green ginger, peeled and chopped
1 Tbs. cornflour	1 Tbs. cornstarch
3 Tbs. light soya sauce	3 Tbs. light soy sauce
1 egg yolk	1 egg yolk
1 tsp. salt	1 tsp. salt
2 Tbs. vegetable oil	2 Tbs. vegetable oil
250ml./8fl.oz. chicken stock	1 cup chicken stock
1 Tbs. rice wine or dry sherry	1 Tbs. rice wine or dry sherry
½kg./1lb. Chinese cabbage, shredded	2½ cups shredded Chinese cabbage

Preheat the oven to moderate 180°C (Gas Mark 4, 350°F).

Put the pork, shallot, water chestnuts, ginger, cornflour (cornstarch), half the soy sauce, egg yolk and salt in a bowl. Mix and knead the mixture until it is well blended, then divide into four pieces. Roll each piece into a ball and set aside.

Heat the oil in a large flameproof casserole. When it is hot, add the pork balls and fry until they are evenly browned. Pour in the remaining soy sauce, stock and wine or sherry and bring to the boil. Cover and transfer the casserole to the oven. Bake for 40 minutes.

Remove from the oven and, using a slotted spoon, remove the pork balls from the casserole. Arrange the cabbage in the casserole and arrange the pork balls on top. Return to the oven and bake for a further 10 to 15 minutes, or until the cabbage is slightly crisp but cooked.

Remove from the oven and serve at once.

Serves 4
Preparation and cooking time: 1¼ hours

Lui Jou-Pien

(Sliced Pork in Wine Sauce)

Metric/Imperial	American
700g./1½lb. pork fillet, cut into 5cm./2in. by 2.5cm./1in. pieces	1½lb. pork tenderloin, cut into 2in. by 1in. pieces
1 tsp. salt	1 tsp. salt
½ tsp. black pepper	½ tsp. black pepper
1 Tbs. soya sauce	1 Tbs. soy sauce
1 Tbs. rice wine or dry sherry	1 Tbs. rice wine or dry sherry
1 Tbs. soya paste	1 Tbs. soy paste
1 Tbs. cornflour	1 Tbs. cornstarch
75ml./3fl.oz. vegetable oil	⅓ cup vegetable oil
SAUCE	SAUCE
15g./½oz. vegetable fat	1 Tbs. vegetable fat
1½ Tbs. spring onion	1½ Tbs. chopped scallion
75ml./3fl.oz. dry white wine	⅓ cup dry white wine
50ml./2fl.oz. chicken stock	¼ cup chicken stock
1 Tbs. soya sauce	1 Tbs. soy sauce
1 tsp. sugar	1 tsp. sugar
¼ tsp. salt	¼ tsp. salt
2 tsp. cornflour, mixed to a paste with 3 Tbs. water	2 tsp. cornstarch, mixed to a paste with 3 Tbs. water

Put the pork slices on a chopping board and sprinkle with the salt, pepper, soy sauce and wine or sherry, rubbing them in gently with your fingers. Add the soy paste and mix evenly with the pork. Dust with the cornflour (cornstarch) and set aside.

Heat the oil in a large frying-pan. When it is hot, add the pork pieces and stir-fry for 2 minutes. Reduce the heat to low and cook the pork for a further 4 minutes, stirring and turning the meat from time to time. Remove from the heat.

To make the sauce, melt the fat in a small saucepan. Add the spring onion (scallion) and cook for 30 seconds, stirring constantly. Add the remaining sauce ingredients except the cornflour (cornstarch) mixture and bring to the boil, stirring frequently. Pour in the cornflour (cornstarch) mixture and cook for 1 minute, stirring frequently, or until the sauce becomes translucent. Remove the pan from the heat and pour the sauce over the pork pieces.

Return the frying-pan containing the pork to high heat and cook for 30 seconds, stirring constantly. Remove from the heat and transfer the mixture to a warmed serving dish. Serve at once.

Serves 4
Preparation and cooking time: 30 minutes

Quick-Fried Spinach with Shredded Pork

Metric/Imperial	American
3 Tbs. vegetable oil	3 Tbs. vegetable oil
225g./8oz. pork fillet, cut across the grain into thin strips	8oz. pork tenderloin, cut across the grain into thin strips
2 Tbs. soya sauce	2 Tbs. soy sauce
1 Tbs. rice wine or dry sherry	1 Tbs. rice wine or dry sherry
1 tsp. sugar	1 tsp. sugar
½ tsp. black pepper	½ tsp. black pepper
40g./1½oz. vegetable fat	3 Tbs. vegetable fat
½kg./1lb. spinach, chopped	2 cups chopped spinach
1 tsp. salt	1 tsp. salt

Heat the oil in a large saucepan. When it is hot, add the pork strips and stir-fry for 2 minutes. Add the soy sauce, wine or sherry, sugar and pepper and stir-fry for a further 2 minutes. Transfer the pork to a plate and set aside.

Add 25g./1oz. (2 tablespoons) of the vegetable fat to the pan and melt it over moderate heat. Add the spinach and salt and stir-fry for 3 minutes. Add the remaining fat to the pan and stir-fry for a further 30 seconds. Using a slotted spoon, transfer the spinach to a warmed serving dish. Increase the heat to moderately high and return the pork strips to the pan. Stir-fry for 1 minute, to reheat them thoroughly.

Remove from the heat and pour the pork strips and juices over the spinach. Serve at once.
Serves 2
Preparation and cooking time: 25 minutes

Sweet and Sour Pork

Metric/Imperial	American
1 Tbs. soya sauce	1 Tbs. soy sauce
1½ Tbs. rice wine or sherry	1½ Tbs. rice wine or sherry
2 Tbs. water	2 Tbs. water
1 egg white, beaten until frothy	1 egg white, beaten until frothy
2 Tbs. cornflour	2 Tbs. cornstarch
½kg./1lb. pork fillet, cut into small cubes or large strips	1lb. pork tenderloin, cut into small cubes or large strips
vegetable oil for deep-frying	vegetable oil for deep-frying
SAUCE	SAUCE
50ml./2fl.oz. peanut oil	¼ cup peanut oil
5cm./2in. piece of fresh root ginger, peeled and chopped	2in. piece of fresh green ginger, peeled and chopped
1 red or green pepper, pith and seeds removed and cut into strips	1 red or green pepper, pith and seeds removed and cut into strips
125g./4oz. tin pineapple chunks	125g./4oz. can pineapple chunks
1 carrot, sliced	1 carrot, sliced
2 Tbs. sugar	2 Tbs. sugar
3 Tbs. wine vinegar	3 Tbs. wine vinegar
2 Tbs. soya sauce	2 Tbs. soy sauce
2 Tbs. tomato purée	2 Tbs. tomato paste

2 tsp. lemon or orange juice	2 tsp. lemon or orange juice
2 Tbs. water	2 Tbs. water
1 Tbs. cornflour	1 Tbs. cornstarch

Combine the soy sauce, wine or sherry, water, egg white and cornflour (cornstarch) to a batter in a large bowl. Stir in the pork pieces until they are well coated, then set aside for 1 hour.

Fill a large saucepan one-third full with oil and heat until it is very hot. Carefully lower the pork pieces into the oil and fry for 3 to 4 minutes, or until they are brown and crisp. Remove from the oil and drain on kitchen towels.

To make the sauce, heat the oil in a large frying-pan. When it is hot, add the ginger and pepper and stir-fry for 2 minutes. Add the pork and all the remaining ingredients except the cornflour (cornstarch) and stir-fry for 2 minutes. Stir in the cornflour (cornstarch) and heat until the sauce has thickened and is translucent. Serve at once.

Serves 4
Preparation and cooking time: 1½ hours

Sweet and Sour Pork, a variation of one of the most famous recipes to come out of China, has a rich, tangy sauce which adds an attractive, translucent sheen.

Run Tsa Li Chi

(Plain Deep-Fried Sliced Pork)

Metric/Imperial	American
700g./1½lb. pork fillet	1½lb. pork tenderloin
2 egg whites	2 egg whites
1½ Tbs. cornflour	1½ Tbs. cornstarch
vegetable oil for deep-frying	vegetable oil for deep-frying
DIP	DIP
1 Tbs. black pepper	1 Tbs. black pepper
1 Tbs. salt	1 Tbs. salt

Slice the pork against the grain into thin slices. Using a mallet, beat the slices until they are very thin, then cut into uniform strips, about 7.5cm./3in. by 5cm./2in. Put the strips into a bowl and set aside.

Beat the egg whites until they are frothy. Gradually beat in the cornflour (cornstarch) until the mixture forms a smooth batter. Pour the batter into the bowl and toss the pork strips until they are thoroughly coated. Set aside for 10 minutes.

Fill a large saucepan one-third full with oil and heat until it is hot. Carefully lower the meat strips, a few at a time, into the oil and fry for 1 minute until they are browned and crisp. Remove from the oil and drain on kitchen towels.

To make the dip, fry the salt and pepper in a small frying-pan over moderately low heat for 4 minutes, stirring constantly. Remove from the heat and transfer the mixture to a small bowl. Serve the pork at once, with the dip.

Serves 4
Preparation and cooking time: 30 minutes

Two simple recipes for pork, Run Tsa Li Chi (above) and Kuo Pa Jou Tin (below), offer a contrast of tastes, the former coated in crisp batter, the latter covered in a delicious sauce.

Kuo Pa Jou Tin

(Diced Pork on Crackling Rice)

Metric/Imperial	American
½kg./1lb. pork fillet, cubed	1lb. pork tenderloin, cubed
salt and pepper to taste	salt and pepper to taste
1½ Tbs. cornflour	1½ Tbs. cornstarch
½kg./1lb. cooked rice	5 cups cooked rice
vegetable oil for deep-frying	vegetable oil for deep-frying
SAUCE	SAUCE
150ml./5fl.oz. chicken stock	⅔ cup chicken stock
3 Tbs. soya sauce	3 Tbs. soy sauce
1 Tbs. sugar	1 Tbs. sugar
2 Tbs. dry sherry	2 Tbs. dry sherry
2 Tbs. corn oil	2 Tbs. corn oil
1 onion, thinly sliced	1 onion, thinly sliced
1 garlic clove, crushed	1 garlic clove, crushed
1½ Tbs. cornflour, mixed to a paste with 4 Tbs. water	1½ Tbs. cornstarch, mixed to a paste with 4 Tbs. water

Preheat the oven to very cool 140°C (Gas Mark 1, 275°F).

Sprinkle the pork with salt, pepper and cornflour (cornstarch), rubbing them into the meat with your fingers. Set aside.

Place the rice in an ovenproof dish and put into the oven. Dry out the rice for 15 to 20 minutes, or until it is crisp.

Heat the oil until is is hot. Carefully lower the pork cubes, a few at a time, into the oil and fry for 3 to 4 minutes or until they are golden. Remove the cubes from the oil and drain on kitchen towels.

To make the sauce, combine the stock, soy sauce, sugar and sherry and set aside.

Heat the oil in a frying-pan. When it is hot, add the onion and garlic and stir-fry for 1 minute. Pour in the stock mixture and bring to the boil. Add the pork, basting well, and reduce the heat to low. Simmer for 2 minutes. Stir in the cornflour (cornstarch) mixture and stir-fry for 2 minutes, or until the sauce has thickened.

Remove the rice from the oven. Return the saucepan with the oil to moderate heat and reheat the oil until it registers 180°C (350°F) on a deep-fat thermometer, or until a small cube of stale bread dropped into the oil turns golden in 55 seconds. Put the rice into a narrow-meshed deep-frying basket and carefully lower it into the oil. Fry for 1½ minutes, then drain on kitchen towels.

Transfer the rice to a warmed serving dish and pour over the pork and sauce.
Serves 4
Preparation and cooking time: 45 minutes

Mi Tse Ho Tui, a leg of gammon (ham), is delicately flavoured with a honey syrup sauce.

Mi Tse Ho Tui

(Ham in Honey Syrup)

Metric/Imperial	American
1 x 1½kg./3lb. middle leg of gammon, washed, soaked in cold water overnight and drained	1 x 3lb. ham, washed, soaked in cold water overnight and drained
SAUCE	SAUCE
2 Tbs. sugar mixed with 4 Tbs. water	2 Tbs. sugar mixed with 4 Tbs. water
2 Tbs. clear honey	2 Tbs. clear honey
2 Tbs. rice wine or sherry	2 Tbs. rice wine or sherry
2 tsp. cherry brandy	2 tsp. cherry brandy
2 tsp. cornflour, mixed to a paste with 3 Tbs. water	2 tsp. cornstarch, mixed to a paste with 3 Tbs. water

Half-fill the lower part of a large steamer with boiling water. Put the gammon (ham) in the upper part and place the steamer over moderate heat. Steam the gammon (ham) for 2¼ hours. Remove from the heat and remove the gammon (ham) from the steamer. Set aside until it is cool enough to handle.

When the gammon (ham) is cool, cut it into ½cm./¼in. slices. Arrange the slices on a heatproof serving dish.

To make the sauce, combine all the ingredients in a saucepan and bring to the boil, stirring constantly. Remove from the heat and pour the sauce evenly over the gammon (ham) slices.

Put the serving dish in the top part of the steamer and return the steamer to moderate heat. Steam the meat and sauce for 3 minutes.

Remove the steamer from the heat and remove the serving dish. Serve at once— the dish should be brought to the table still wreathed in steam.
Serves 6-8
Preparation and cooking time: 14½ hours

Double Cooked Pork

Metric/Imperial	American
1 x 2kg./2lb. lean belly of pork	1 x 2lb. lean belly or bacon of pork
50ml./2fl.oz. vegetable oil	¼ cup vegetable oil
1 large green pepper, pith and seeds removed and cut into thin strips	1 large green pepper, pith and seeds removed and cut into thin strips
1 red pepper, pith and seeds removed and cut into thin strips	1 red pepper, pith and seeds removed and cut into thin strips
3 garlic cloves, crushed	3 garlic cloves, crushed
3 spring onions, chopped	3 scallions, chopped
1 chilli, chopped	1 chilli, chopped
1½ Tbs. bean paste	1½ Tbs. bean paste
2 tsp. sugar	2 tsp. sugar
2 Tbs. rice wine or sherry	2 Tbs. rice wine or sherry

Put the pork into a large saucepan and cover with water. Bring to the boil, cover and simmer for 1 hour, or until the pork is cooked through. Drain and rinse in cold water. When it is cool enough to handle, chop or cut through the lean and fat into thin strips.

Heat half the oil in a frying-pan. When it is very hot, add the pork pieces and stir-fry for 5 minutes. Remove the pan from the heat, transfer the pork to a dish and drain off the oil.

Add the remaining oil to the pan. When it is very hot, add the peppers, garlic and spring onions (scallions) and stir-fry for 2 minutes. Add the pork, chilli and bean paste and stir-fry for 1 minute. Stir in the remaining ingredients and stir-fry until they are heated through. Serve at once.

Serves 4
Preparation and cooking time: 1½ hours

Jou Ping Hui Por-Ts'Ai

(Fried and Baked Pork Cakes with Spinach)

Metric/Imperial	American
½kg./1lb. lean pork, minced	1lb. lean pork, ground
2 medium onions, chopped	2 medium onions, chopped
1 egg	1 egg
2 Tbs. cornflour	2 Tbs. cornstarch
2 tsp. sugar	2 tsp. sugar
2½ Tbs. soya sauce	2½ Tbs. soy sauce
1 Tbs. tomato purée	1 Tbs. tomato paste
1 tsp. salt	1 tsp. salt
¼ tsp. black pepper	¼ tsp. black pepper
vegetable oil for deep-frying	vegetable oil for deep-frying
25g./1oz. vegetable fat	2 Tbs. vegetable fat
25g./1oz. butter	2 Tbs. butter
½kg./1lb. spinach, chopped	2½ cups chopped spinach

Combine the pork, onions, egg, cornflour (cornstarch), 1 teaspoon of sugar, 1½ tablespoons of soy sauce, the tomato purée (paste), half the salt and the pepper until they are well blended. Shape the mixture into four or six balls, then press the balls down to form patties about 7.5cm./3in. in diameter.

Fill a large saucepan one-third full with oil and heat until it is hot. Put two or three of the patties into a deep-frying basket and carefully lower them into the the oil. Fry for 3 to 4 minutes, or until they are lightly and evenly browned. Remove from the oil and drain on kitchen towels.

Preheat the oven to hot 220°C (Gas Mark 7, 425°F).

Melt the vegetable fat with half the butter in a large frying-pan. Add the spinach and fry for 1 minute, stirring constantly. Add the remaining salt, the remaining sugar and the remaining soy sauce and fry for a further 3 minutes, stirring constantly. Remove from the heat.

Spread the spinach over the bottom of a casserole dish and arrange the meat cakes on top. Cut the remaining butter into small pieces and dot over the tops of the cakes. Cover the casserole and put it into the oven. Bake for 8 minutes.

Remove from the oven and serve at once.

Serves 4-6
Preparation and cooking time: 40 minutes

Jou Yuants'a Hui

(Meatball Chop Suey)

Metric/Imperial	American
350g./12oz. lean pork, minced	12oz. lean pork, ground
50g./2oz. water chestnuts, finely chopped	⅓ cup finely chopped water chestnuts
1 small egg	1 small egg
½ tsp. sugar	½ tsp. sugar
½ tsp. salt	½ tsp. salt
¼ tsp. white pepper	¼ tsp. white pepper
1 Tbs. soya sauce	1 Tbs. soy sauce
1 Tbs. cornflour	1 Tbs. cornstarch
vegetable oil for deep-frying	vegetable oil for deep-frying
2 Tbs. vegetable oil	2 Tbs. vegetable oil
2 medium onions, thinly sliced	2 medium onions, thinly sliced
225g./8oz. cabbage, shredded	1½ cups shredded cabbage
300ml./10fl.oz. chicken stock	1¼ cups chicken stock
225g./8oz. bean sprouts	1 cup bean sprouts
¼ small cucumber, shredded	¼ small cucumber, shredded

Combine the pork, water chestnuts, egg, sugar, salt, pepper, soy sauce and corn-flour (cornstarch) until they are well blended. Form the mixture into 10 or 12 small balls.

Fill a large saucepan one-third full with vegetable oil and heat until it is hot. Carefully arrange a few of the meatballs in a deep-frying basket and lower them into the oil. Fry for 3 to 4 minutes, or until they are lightly browned. Remove from the oil and drain. Keep hot while you cook the remaining meatballs.

Heat the vegetable oil in a flameproof casserole. When it is hot, add the onions and cabbage and cook, stirring occasionally, until the vegetables are soft. Pour in the stock and bring to the boil. Reduce the heat to low and simmer the mixture, stirring occasionally, for 5 minutes. Spread the bean sprouts evenly over the vegetable mixture, then top with the shredded cucumber. Arrange the meatballs on top of the vegetables. Simmer the mixture for 5 to 8 minutes, or until the meatballs have been heated through.

Remove from the heat and serve at once.

Serves 4
Preparation and cooking time: 1 hour

POULTRY

Chicken with Broccoli and Walnuts

Metric/Imperial	American
2 large chicken breasts, boned and cut into small cubes	2 large chicken breasts, boned and cut into small cubes
1 tsp. salt	1 tsp. salt
1 tsp. ground ginger	1 tsp. ground ginger
2 Tbs. cornflour	2 Tbs. cornstarch
1 large egg white, lightly beaten	1 large egg white, lightly beaten
75ml./3fl.oz. peanut oil	$\frac{1}{3}$ cup peanut oil
4 large broccoli spears, cut into small pieces	4 large broccoli spears, cut into small pieces
225g./8oz. shelled walnuts, halved	2 cups shelled halved walnuts
1 tsp. soft brown sugar	1 tsp. soft brown sugar
2 Tbs. soya sauce	2 Tbs. soy sauce
3 Tbs. rice wine or dry sherry	3 Tbs. rice wine or dry sherry

Rub the chicken cubes first with the salt, then the ginger and finally with the cornflour (cornstarch). Transfer them to a bowl and pour over the beaten egg white. Stir around gently so that all the cubes are coated.

Heat the oil in a large frying-pan. When it is very hot, add the chicken cubes and stir-fry over moderately high heat for 3 minutes. Using a slotted spoon, transfer the cubes to a plate and keep hot.

Add the broccoli pieces and walnuts to the pan and stir-fry for 3 minutes. Return the chicken cubes to the pan and stir-fry for 1 minute, or until they are well blended.

Stir in the sugar, soy sauce and wine or sherry and cook for 1½ minutes. Transfer the mixture to a warmed serving bowl and serve at once.

Serves 4

Preparation and cooking time: 30 minutes

Kuo Tieh Chi (Egg-Braised Sliced Chicken) is exquisitely flavoured with a blend of parsley, sherry, soy sauce and lemon juice.

Kuo Tieh Chi

(Egg-Braised Sliced Chicken)

Metric/Imperial	American
350g./12oz. boned chicken breasts, cut into thin strips	1½ cups boned chicken breasts, cut into thin strips
salt and pepper	salt and pepper
2 tsp. sugar	2 tsp. sugar
1 tsp. chilli sauce	1 tsp. chilli sauce
2 Tbs. dry white wine	2 Tbs. dry white wine
1 Tbs. cornflour	1 Tbs. cornstarch
vegetable oil for deep-frying	vegetable oil for deep-frying
3 eggs, lightly beaten	3 eggs, lightly beaten
75ml./3fl.oz. sesame oil	⅓ cup sesame oil
1 Tbs. chopped parsley	1 Tbs. chopped parsley
1½ Tbs. dry sherry	1½ Tbs. dry sherry
1½ Tbs. soya sauce	1½ Tbs. soy sauce
1½ Tbs. lemon juice	1½ Tbs. lemon juice

Rub the chicken strips with the salt, pepper, sugar, chilli sauce, wine and corn-flour (cornstarch). Set aside at room temperature for 1½ hours.

Fill a large saucepan about one-third full with oil and heat until it is hot. Carefully lower the chicken strips, a few at a time, into the oil and fry for 1 to 2 minutes, or until they are golden. Drain on kitchen towels.

Put the eggs in a shallow bowl. Dip the cooked chicken strips in the eggs and coat thickly.

Heat the sesame oil in a large frying-pan. When it is hot, add the strips to the pan, in one layer if possible. Shake and tilt to distribute the oil evenly and, turning occasionally, fry for 2 minutes or until the strips are golden brown.

Transfer to a large, warmed serving dish and sprinkle over the parsley, sherry, soy sauce and lemon juice.

Serves 4
Preparation and cooking time: 2 hours

Lemon Chicken

Metric/Imperial	American
1 x 2kg./4lb. chicken, skinned	1 x 4lb. chicken, skinned
1½ tsp. salt	1½ tsp. salt
2.5cm./1in. piece of fresh root ginger, peeled and grated	1in. piece of fresh green ginger, peeled and grated
1 egg, lightly beaten	1 egg, lightly beaten
125g./4oz. ground rice	1 cup ground rice
vegetable oil for deep-frying	vegetable oil for deep-frying
juice of 1 lemon	juice of 1 lemon
1 spring onion, chopped	1 scallion, chopped
1 lemon, cut into thin slices	1 lemon, cut into thin slices
SAUCE	SAUCE
75ml./3fl.oz. chicken stock	⅓ cup chicken stock
2 Tbs. rice wine or dry sherry	2 Tbs. rice wine or dry sherry
¼ tsp. salt	¼ tsp. salt
1½ tsp. sugar	1½ tsp. sugar

Cut the chicken, using a cleaver, through the bone, into 20 or 24 pieces. Sprinkle the pieces with salt and ginger, rubbing them into the flesh.

Dip the chicken pieces in the beaten egg one by one, then roll in the ground rice until they are thoroughly coated, shaking off any excess.

Fill a large saucepan one-third full with oil and heat until it is very hot. Carefully lower a few of the chicken pieces into the oil and fry for 3 to 5 minutes, or until they are golden brown and crisp. Remove from the oil and drain on kitchen towels.

To make the sauce, put all the ingredients in a small saucepan and bring to the boil. Remove from the heat and pour over the chicken pieces.

Sprinkle the lemon juice and spring onion (scallion) over the chicken. Arrange the lemon slices around the chicken and serve at once.

Serves 4-6
Preparation and cooking time: 40 minutes

Yu-lang-chi

(Chicken and Ham)

Metric/Imperial	American
1¾l./3 pints chicken stock	7½ cups chicken stock
4cm./1½in. piece of fresh root ginger, peeled and chopped	1½in. piece of fresh green ginger, peeled and chopped
3 spring onions, chopped	3 scallions, chopped
1 x 2kg./4lb. chicken	1 x 4lb. chicken
4 slices prosciutto	4 slices prosciutto
700g./1½lb. broccoli spears	1½lb. broccoli spears
1 Tbs. soya sauce	1 Tbs. soy sauce
1 tsp. cornflour, blended to a paste with 1 Tbs. water	1 tsp. cornstarch, blended to a paste with 1 Tbs. water

Put the stock, ginger and spring onions (scallions) into a large saucepan. Bring to the boil, then add the chicken and enough boiling water to cover the chicken. Return to the boil. Reduce the heat to low, cover the pan and simmer the chicken for 40 minutes.

Remove from the heat and set aside, covered, for 2 hours. (The chicken will cook through during this time.)

Remove the chicken from the stock, reserving about 450ml./15fl.oz. (2 cups) of it. Put the chicken on a chopping board, remove the flesh from the bones, discarding the skin, and cut into serving pieces. Arrange the chicken pieces and ham strips on a warmed serving dish.

Strain the reserved stock and return it to the saucepan. Bring to the boil, then add the broccoli spears. Return to the boil.

Remove the pan from the heat and set aside for 5 minutes. Drain the broccoli, reserving 125ml./4fl.oz. (½ cup) of stock. Arrange the broccoli around the chicken and ham mixture.

Combine the reserved stock and soy sauce, then pour into a small saucepan. Bring to the boil. Add the cornflour (cornstarch) mixture and cook, stirring constantly, until the sauce thickens a little and becomes translucent.

Pour the sauce over the chicken and ham and serve at once.
Serves 6
Preparation and cooking time: 3 hours

Pai chou chi

(White Cooked Chicken)

Metric/Imperial	American
2.5l./4 pints water	2½ quarts water
1 x 2kg./4lb. chicken, cleaned	1 x 4lb. chicken, cleaned
6 spring onions, finely chopped	6 scallions, finely chopped
SAUCE A	SAUCE A
5cm./2in. piece of fresh root ginger, peeled and chopped	2in. piece of fresh green ginger, peeled and chopped
4 Tbs. boiling water	4 Tbs. boiling water
1 Tbs. hot oil	1 Tbs. hot oil
½ tsp. salt	½ tsp. salt
SAUCE B	SAUCE B
2 garlic cloves, crushed	2 garlic cloves, crushed
3 Tbs. soya sauce	3 Tbs. soy sauce
2 Tbs. vinegar	2 Tbs. vinegar

Yu Lang Chi is tender chicken and ham on a bed of fresh, green broccoli. Serve with steamed rice for a satisfying meal.

Pour the water into a saucepan and bring to the boil. Add the chicken and return the water to the boil. Reduce the heat to low and simmer the chicken for 1¼ hours. Remove from the heat, cover and allow to cool for 3 hours.

Drain the chicken, discarding the cooking liquid, and transfer it to a chopping board. Chop the chicken, through the bone, into about 20 large-bite pieces. Transfer the pieces to a serving plate and set aside.

To make sauce A, put the chopped ginger into a small serving bowl. Add all the remaining ingredients and stir to blend.

To make sauce B, put the garlic into a small serving bowl. Add the remaining ingredients and stir to blend.

Sprinkle the chopped spring onions (scallions) over the chicken pieces and serve at once, with sauces.

Serves 4
Preparation and cooking time: $4\frac{1}{2}$ hours

Hung Shao Chi (Red-Cooked Chicken) adds colour and a delicate quality to chicken.

Hung Shao Chi

(Red-Cooked Chicken)

You can either use a roasting chicken for this dish, or a cheaper boiling chicken. If you use the latter, increase the cooking time by about 30 minutes.

Metric/Imperial	American
2 spring onions, cut into 5cm./2in. lengths	2 scallions, cut into 2in. lengths
4cm./1½in. piece of fresh root ginger, peeled and sliced	1½in. piece of fresh green ginger, peeled and sliced
1 x 1½kg./3lb. chicken	1 x 3lb. chicken
75ml./3fl.oz. vegetable oil	⅓ cup vegetable oil
75ml./3fl.oz. soya sauce	⅓ cup soy sauce
300ml./10fl.oz. water	1¼ cups water

½ chicken stock cube, crumbled	½ chicken bouillon cube, crumbled
2 tsp. sugar	2 tsp. sugar
3 Tbs. sherry	3 Tbs. sherry

Stuff the spring onions (scallions) and ginger into the cavity of the chicken and secure it with a skewer or trussing needle and thread.

Heat the oil in a large saucepan. When it is hot, arrange the chicken in the pan and fry it, turning frequently, until it is evenly browned. Remove from the heat and pour off the excess oil.

Add the soy sauce, water, stock (bouillon) cube, sugar and sherry and stir to blend. Return the pan to the heat and bring the mixture to the boil. Cover the pan, reduce the heat to low and simmer for 30 minutes. Turn the chicken over, re-cover the pan and simmer for a further 45 minutes, or until the chicken is cooked through and tender.

Transfer the chicken to a carving board. Untruss and carve into serving pieces. Transfer the pieces to a warmed serving dish and pour over the cooking liquid. Serve at once.
Serves 4
Preparation and cooking time: 1½ hours

Pai Chiu Tung Chi

(Long-Simmered Chicken in White Wine)

The cooking liquid from this dish is sometimes served separately as a soup course.

Metric/Imperial	American
1 x 2kg./4lb. chicken, cleaned	1 x 4lb. chicken, cleaned
600ml./1 pint water	2½ cups water
300ml./10fl.oz. dry white wine	1¼ cups dry white wine
3 Tbs. soya sauce	3 Tbs. soy sauce
1½ Tbs. sesame oil	1½ Tbs. sesame oil
½kg./1lb. Chinese cabbage, shredded	2½ cups shredded Chinese cabbage
STUFFING	STUFFING
75g./3oz. long-grain rice, soaked in cold water for 30 minutes and drained	⅓ cup long-grain rice, soaked in cold water for 30 minutes and drained
4 spring onions, chopped	4 scallions, chopped
4 lean bacon slices, chopped	4 Canadian bacon slices, chopped
5cm./2in. piece of fresh root ginger, peeled and chopped	2in. piece of fresh green ginger, peeled and chopped
1 chicken stock cube, crumbled	1 chicken bouillon cube, crumbled
salt and white pepper to taste	salt and white pepper to taste

Preheat the oven to cool 150°C (Gas Mark 2, 300°F).

To make the stuffing, combine all the ingredients in a bowl, then stuff into the cavity of the chicken. Close with a skewer or trussing needle and thread.

Put the chicken in a flameproof casserole and pour over the water. Bring to the boil, and transfer the casserole to the oven. Bake the chicken for 1 hour. Add the wine and cook the chicken for a further 45 minutes, or until it is cooked through and tender. Remove from the oven and transfer the chicken to a warmed serving dish. Keep hot.

Combine the soy sauce and sesame oil and pour the mixture over the chicken. Serve at once. To serve the cooking liquid as a soup course, stir in the cabbage and bring to the boil, stirring occasionally. Cook for 5 minutes, then serve at once.
Serves 4-6
Preparation and cooking time: 2¾ hours

Sweet and Sour Chicken

Thinly sliced chicken breasts combine with a tasty assortment of vegetables and a piquant sweet-sour sauce to make this mouthwatering dish of Sweet and Sour Chicken.

Metric/Imperial	American
½ tsp. salt	½ tsp. salt
1 tsp. cornflour	1 tsp. cornstarch
2 chicken breasts, boned and cut into thin strips	2 chicken breasts, boned and cut into thin strips
4 Tbs. corn oil	4 Tbs. corn oil
25g./1oz. bamboo shoots, chopped	3 Tbs. chopped bamboo shoots
1 green pepper, pith and seeds removed and finely chopped	1 green pepper, pith and seeds removed and finely chopped
1 small onion, chopped	1 small onion, chopped
4cm./1½in. piece of fresh root ginger, peeled and finely chopped	1½in. piece of fresh green ginger, peeled and finely chopped
1 garlic clove, chopped	1 garlic clove, chopped
SAUCE	SAUCE
1 Tbs. soya sauce	1 Tbs. soy sauce
1 Tbs. red wine vinegar	1 Tbs. red wine vinegar
1 Tbs. soft brown sugar	1 Tbs. soft brown sugar
1 Tbs. tomato purée	1 Tbs. tomato paste
4 Tbs. chicken stock	4 Tbs. chicken stock

Mix the salt and cornflour (cornstarch) together and gently rub into the chicken strips with your fingertips.

Heat the oil in a large frying-pan. When it is very hot, add the chicken, in one layer if possible, and stir-fry for 4 minutes. Remove the strips from the pan and drain on kitchen towels. Set aside and keep warm.

Add the bamboo shoots, pepper, onion, ginger and garlic and stir-fry for 1 minute. Mix all the sauce ingredients together in a small bowl.

Return the chicken strips to the pan, with the sauce. Cook for 1 minute, or until all the strips and vegetables are well coated with the sauce.

Transfer to a warmed tureen and serve.

Serves 4
Preparation and cooking time: 20 minutes

Quick-Fried Chicken cubes in White Sauce

Metric/Imperial	American
4 chicken breasts, boned	4 chicken breasts, boned
1 tsp. ground ginger	1 tsp. ground ginger
1½ tsp. salt	1½ tsp. salt
1 tsp. black pepper	1 tsp. black pepper
1 Tbs. cornflour	1 Tbs. cornstarch
15g./½oz. butter	1 Tbs. butter
2 Tbs. vegetable oil	2 Tbs. vegetable oil
125g./4oz. shelled shrimps	⅔ cup peeled shrimp
1 small red pepper, pith and seeds removed and cut into 1cm./½in. lengths	1 small red pepper, pith and seeds removed and cut into ½in. lengths
½ cucumber, halved and cut into 1cm./½in. lengths	½ cucumber, halved and cut into ½in. lengths
SAUCE	SAUCE
75ml./3fl.oz. chicken stock	⅓ cup chicken stock
15g./½oz. butter	1 Tbs. butter
50ml./2fl.oz. dry white wine	¼ cup dry white wine
1 Tbs. cornflour, mixed to a paste with 4 Tbs. water	1 Tbs. cornstarch, mixed to a paste with 4 Tbs. water
125ml./4fl.oz. single cream	½ cup light cream

Cut the chicken flesh into small cubes, then rub them with ginger, salt, pepper and cornflour (cornstarch). Set aside.

Melt the butter with the oil in a large frying-pan. Add the chicken cubes and stir-fry for 30 seconds. Add the shrimps, pepper and cucumber and stir-fry for 2 minutes. Remove from the heat and set aside.

To make the sauce, bring the stock to the boil in a small saucepan. Stir in the butter and wine and boil until the butter has melted. Reduce the heat to low and stir in the cornflour (cornstarch) mixture. Simmer for 2 minutes, stirring constantly, until the sauce has thickened. Stir in the cream.

Remove from the heat and pour the sauce over the chicken cubes. Return the frying-pan to moderate heat and cook the mixture, turning the meat and vegetables in the sauce, for 2 minutes.

Transfer the mixture to a warmed serving dish and serve at once.
Serves 4
Preparation and cooking time: 30 minutes

White Cut Chicken

Metric/Imperial	American
1.2l./2 pints chicken stock	5 cups chicken stock
1 Tbs. rice wine or dry sherry	1 Tbs. rice wine or dry sherry
50ml./2fl.oz. soya sauce	¼ cup soy sauce
4 spring onions, cut into 2.5cm./1in. lengths	4 scallions, cut into 1in. lengths
2.5cm./1in. piece of fresh root ginger, peeled and sliced	1½in. piece of fresh green peeled and sliced
1 tsp. sugar	1 tsp. sugar
1 tsp. salt	1 tsp. salt
1 x 2kg./4lb. chicken, oven-ready	1 x 4lb. chicken, oven-ready

Put the stock, wine or sherry, 1 tablespoon of soy sauce, the spring onions (scallions), ginger, sugar and salt in a large saucepan and bring to the boil. Reduce the heat to low and add the chicken. Cover and simmer for 30 minutes.

Remove from the heat and set aside for 2 hours, or until the chicken has cooled completely. Remove from the pan and discard the cooking liquid. Remove and discard the skin from the chicken and cut the flesh into 5cm./2in. pieces. Transfer the pieces to a serving dish.

Pour the remaining soy sauce into a bowl. Serve the chicken immediately, accompanied by the soy sauce.

Serves 6
Preparation and cooking time: 3 hours

Steamed Drumsticks

Metric/Imperial	American
12 chicken drumsticks	12 chicken drumsticks
5cm./2in. piece of fresh root ginger, peeled and chopped	2in. piece of fresh green ginger, peeled and chopped
6 spring onions, cut into 5cm./2in. lengths	6 scallions, cut into 2in. lengths
1 tsp. salt	1 tsp. salt
1 tsp. butter	1 tsp. butter
25g./1oz. vegetable fat	2 Tbs. vegetable fat
1 medium onion, chopped	1 medium onion, chopped
2 tsp. sugar	2 tsp. sugar
¼ tsp. cayenne pepper	¼ tsp. cayenne pepper
½ tsp. 5-spice powder	½ tsp. 5-spice powder
1 Tbs. soya sauce	1 Tbs. soy sauce
1 tsp. chilli sauce	1 tsp. chilli sauce
2 Tbs. tomato purée	2 Tbs. tomato paste
125ml./4fl.oz. chicken stock	½ cup chicken stock
2 tsp. cornflour, mixed to a paste with 1 Tbs. stock	2 tsp. cornstarch, mixed to a paste with 1 Tbs. stock

Half-fill a large saucepan with water and bring to the boil. Add the drumsticks and boil for 2 minutes. Remove the pan from the heat and drain the drumsticks on kitchen towels. Transfer to a large basin. Add the ginger and spring onions (scallions) and sprinkle over half the salt. Cut out circles of greaseproof or waxed paper and foil and grease with the butter. Make a pleat across the centre and put the paper circle, greased side down, over the basin; tie securely with string. Put the basin into a large saucepan and pour in enough boiling water to come halfway up the sides. Cover the pan and set over low heat. Steam the chicken for 45 minutes to 1 hour, depending on the size of the drumsticks.

Meanwhile, melt the fat in a large frying-pan. When it is hot, add the onion and stir-fry for 2 minutes. Add the sugar, cayenne, 5-spice powder, soy sauce, chilli sauce, tomato purée (paste), stock and remaining salt and bring to the boil, stirring constantly. Add the cornflour (cornstarch) mixture and cook, stirring constantly, until the sauce thickens and becomes translucent. Remove from the heat and keep hot.

Remove the saucepan from the heat and lift the basin out of the pan. Remove and discard the paper circles. Transfer the mixture to a warmed serving dish.

Pour the chicken cooking liquids into the sauce and stir well to blend. Pour the sauce over the chicken mixture and serve at once.

Serves 6
Preparation and cooking time: 1½ hours

Chicken Congee

Metric/Imperial	American
1 x 1½kg./3lb. chicken	1 x 3lb. chicken
1.75l./3 pints water	7½ cups water
1 onion, quartered	1 onion, quartered
12 peppercorns	12 peppercorns
2 bay leaves	2 bay leaves
125g./4oz. long-grain rice, soaked in cold water for 30 minutes and drained	⅔ cup long-grain rice, soaked in cold water for 30 minutes and drained
GARNISH	GARNISH
½ small Chinese cabbage, shredded	½ small Chinese cabbage, shredded
4 spring onions, chopped	4 scallions, chopped
125ml./4fl.oz. soya sauce	½ cup soy sauce

Put the chicken into a large saucepan and pour over the water. Add the onion and flavourings and bring to the boil. Reduce the heat to low, cover the pan and simmer for 1 to 1½ hours, or until the chicken is cooked through. Transfer the chicken to a chopping board, strain the cooking liquid and reserve it.

Put the rice into a saucepan and pour over the stock. Bring to the boil, cover and simmer the mixture for 1 hour.

Meanwhile, when the chicken is cool enough to handle, skin and chop the meat into bite-sized pieces. Divide the meat into light or dark and put half of both into the saucepan with the rice. Simmer for a further 15 minutes.

Meanwhile, arrange the remaining chicken pieces in separate bowls, for light and dark meat, and arrange the garnishes in appropriate serving bowls.

Remove the pan from the heat and pour the mixture into a warmed tureen. Serve at once, with the meat and garnishes.
Serves 6
Preparation and cooking time: 3½ hours

Stir-Fry Duck with Ginger and Pineapple

Metric/Imperial	American
1 x 2kg./4lb. duck	1 x 4lb. duck
pepper to taste	pepper to taste
1 tsp. ground ginger	1 tsp. ground ginger
5 Tbs. soya sauce	5 Tbs. soy sauce
50ml./2fl.oz. vegetable oil	¼ cup vegetable oil
12.5cm./5in. piece of fresh root ginger, peeled and chopped	5in. piece of fresh green ginger, peeled and chopped
2 spring onions, chopped	2 scallions, chopped
1 Tbs. soft brown sugar	1 Tbs. soft brown sugar
2 Tbs. wine vinegar	2 Tbs. wine vinegar
225g./8oz. can pineapple chunks with the can juice reserved	8oz. pineapple chunks, with the can juice reserved
1 Tbs. cornflour, mixed to a paste with 2 Tbs. water	1 Tbs. cornstarch, mixed to a paste with 2 Tbs. water

Preheat the oven to warm 170°C (Gas Mark 3, 325°F).

Put the duck on the rack of a roasting pan. Mix the pepper, ground ginger and half of the soy sauce together and brush over the duck. Put into the oven and roast for 2 to 2½ hours, basting frequently with the pan juices, or until the duck is cooked through and tender, and the skin is crisp. Remove from the oven and set aside until it is cool enough to handle. Using a cleaver, chop the duck, through the skin, into bite-sized pieces.

Heat the oil in a large, deep frying-pan. When it is hot, add the chopped ginger and stir-fry for 1 minute. Add the duck pieces and spring onions (scallions), and stir-fry for 1 minute. Add the soy sauce, sugar, vinegar and pineapple chunks and can juice. Bring to the boil and cook for 2 minutes, stirring occasionally.

Stir in the cornflour (cornstarch) mixture and cook, stirring constantly, until the sauce thickens and becomes translucent. Transfer the mixture to a warmed serving dish and serve at once.

Serves 6
Preparation and cooking time: 3 hours

Yun Yook

(Roasted Wood Pigeons)

Metric/Imperial	American
2 Tbs. chilli oil	2 Tbs. chilli oil
4 slices streaky bacon	4 slices fatty bacon
4 young wood pigeons, oven-ready	4 young wood pigeons, oven-ready
12 vine leaves	12 vine leaves
125g./4oz. sultanas	$\frac{2}{3}$ cup seedless raisins
8 mint leaves	8 mint leaves
10 pickling onions, boiled for 5 minutes and drained	10 pearl onions, boiled for 5 minutes and drained
225g./8oz. button mushrooms	2 cups button mushrooms
2 Tbs. olive oil	2 Tbs. olive oil
salt and pepper to taste	salt and pepper to taste
2 Tbs. chopped parsley or coriander	2 Tbs. chopped parsley or coriander

Preheat the oven to moderate 180°C (Gas Mark 4, 350°F).

Heat the oil in a frying-pan. When it is hot, add the bacon and fry until it is crisp. Remove the pan from the heat and set aside.

Put the pigeons on a flat surface. Lay one bacon slice over the breast of each one and cover each pigeon with three vine leaves, so that they overlap or enclose the pigeons. Secure with cocktail sticks or trussing thread. Arrange the pigeons in a casserole large enough to hold them in one layer. Add the sultanas (seedless raisins), mint leaves, onions and mushrooms, olive oil and salt and pepper to taste. Cover and put into the oven. Cook for 25 to 30 minutes or until the pigeons are cooked through and tender.

Remove the casserole from the oven, remove the sticks or trussing thread and sprinkle over the parsley or coriander. Serve at once.

Serves 4
Preparation and cooking time: 1 hour

Mongolian Steamboat

Metric/Imperial	American
1 x 2kg./4lb. roasting chicken	1 x 4lb. roasting chicken
1 medium onion, chopped	1 medium onion, chopped

1 bouquet garni
10 peppercorns
2 bay leaves
1 tsp. salt
1.2l./2 pints water
175g./6oz. crabmeat
175g./6oz. large prawns, shelled
VEGETABLES
125g./4oz. mushrooms, sliced
1 red pepper, pith and seeds removed and
   sliced
1 green pepper, pith and seeds removed
   and sliced
175g./6oz. Chinese cabbage, shredded
125g./4oz. canned lotus root, drained and
   sliced
GARNISHES
275g./10oz. cooked rice
4 Tbs. chopped spring onion
10cm./4in. piece of fresh root ginger,
   peeled and finely chopped

1 bouquet garni
10 peppercorns
2 bay leaves
1 tsp. salt
5 cups water
6oz. crabmeat
1 cup large peeled shrimp
VEGETABLES
1 cup sliced mushrooms
1 red pepper, pith and seeds removed
   and sliced
1 green pepper, pith and seeds removed
   and sliced
1 cup shredded Chinese cabbage
4oz. canned lotus root, drained and
   sliced
GARNISHES
4 cups cooked rice
4 Tbs. chopped scallion
4in. piece of fresh green ginger, peeled
   and finely chopped

(See over) The cooking liquid of wine and stock used to steam Pai Chiu Tung Li Yu can be made into a savoury soup.

Remove the skin, bones and flesh from the chicken. Set the flesh aside and put the skin, bones and giblets into a saucepan with the onion, bouquet garni, peppercorns, bay leaves, salt and water. Bring to the boil, skimming off any scum from the surface. Reduce the heat to low, cover and simmer the stock for 1 to 1½ hours. Remove from the heat and strain the stock. Set aside.

Meanwhile, prepare the meat and fish. Cut the chicken flesh into bite-sized pieces and arrange decoratively on a large serving platter. Cut the crabmeat and prawns (shrimp) into bite-sized pieces and arrange with the chicken.

To prepare the vegetables, arrange them attractively on a large serving platter and set them aside with the meat and fish.

Put all the garnishes into separate bowls and arrange with the other dishes.

Put the firepot or fondue pot in the centre of the table and arrange the various platters around it. Bring the stock to the boil in a saucepan and pour into the fondue pot. Light the spirit burner. The food is now ready to be cooked, in the same way as fondue.
Serves 6
Preparation and cooking time: 2½ hours

Derived from an ancient Cantonese recipe, succulent young wood pigeons wrapped in vine leaves result in Yun Yook, a dish for special occasions.

FISH

Pai Chiu Tung Li Yu

(Carp Steamed in White Wine)

Metric/Imperial	American
1 x 1½kg./3lb. carp, cleaned and gutted	1 x 3lb. carp, cleaned and gutted
150ml./5fl.oz. water	⅔ cup water
150ml./5fl.oz. beef stock	⅔ cup beef stock
300ml./10fl.oz. dry white wine	1¼ cups dry white wine
3 Tbs. soya sauce	3 Tbs. soy sauce
1½ Tbs. sesame oil	1½ Tbs. sesame oil
1 bunch of watercress, shredded	1 bunch of watercress, shredded
STUFFING	STUFFING
4 Tbs. rice, soaked in cold water and drained	4 Tbs. rice, soaked in cold water and drained
4 slices lean bacon, chopped	4 slices Canadian bacon, chopped
4 spring onions, finely chopped	4 scallions, finely chopped
1 chicken stock cube, crumbled	1 chicken bouillon cube, crumbled
7.5cm./3in. piece of fresh root ginger, peeled and finely chopped	3in. piece of fresh green ginger, peeled and finely chopped
salt and pepper to taste	salt and pepper to taste

To make the stuffing, combine all the ingredients and stuff the mixture into the fish. Close the cavity with a skewer or trussing needle and thread.

Put the carp into an oval-shaped heatproof casserole and pour over the water. Fill the bottom part of a double boiler or steamer to a depth of 5cm./2in. with boiling water. Put the casserole in the top part and cover. Place the boiler or steamer over moderate heat and steam for 45 minutes.

Pour the stock and wine into the casserole and steam for a further 45 minutes or until the fish flesh flakes easily. Transfer the fish to a warmed dish and reserve the cooking liquid.

Combine the soy sauce and sesame oil and pour over the fish before serving.

To serve the cooking liquid as a soup, stir in the watercress and bring to the boil. Boil for 2 minutes before serving.

Serves 4-6
Preparation and cooking time: 1¾ hours

Liu Yu-pien

(Sliced Fish in Wine Sauce)

Metric/Imperial	American
575g./1¼lb. sole fillets, cut into 5cm./2in. by 2.5cm./1in. pieces	1¼lb. sole fillets, cut into 2in. by 1in. pieces
1 tsp. salt	1 tsp. salt
½ tsp. black pepper	½ tsp. black pepper
½ tsp. ground ginger	½ tsp. ground ginger
2 tsp. cornflour	2 tsp. cornstarch
1 egg white, lightly beaten	1 egg white, lightly beaten
75ml./3fl.oz. vegetable oil	⅓ cup vegetable oil
SAUCE	SAUCE
2 tsp. vegetable fat	2 tsp. vegetable fat
50g./2oz. dried mushrooms, soaked in	½ cup dried mushrooms, soaked in cold

cold water for 30 minutes, drained and sliced

75ml./3fl.oz. dry white wine

50ml./2fl.oz. chicken stock

1 tsp. sugar

½ tsp. salt

2 tsp. cornflour, mixed to a paste with 3 Tbs. water

water for 30 minutes, drained and sliced

⅓ cup dry white wine

¼ cup chicken stock

1 tsp. sugar

½ tsp. salt

2 tsp. cornstarch, mixed to a paste with 3 Tbs. water

Put the fish pieces on a chopping board and sprinkle with the salt, pepper, ginger and cornflour (cornstarch), rubbing them into the flesh with your fingers. Pour over the egg white and gently toss to coat thoroughly. Set aside.

Heat the oil in a large frying-pan. When it is hot, add the fish pieces, in one layer if possible. Cook for 30 seconds, tilting the pan so that the oil flows around the fish. Turn and cook for a further 1 minute. Remove the pan from the heat and pour off the excess oil. Set aside.

To prepare the sauce, melt the fat in a small saucepan. Add the mushrooms and cook for 1 minute, stirring constantly. Add the wine, stock, sugar and salt and bring to the boil. Stir in the cornflour (cornstarch) mixture and cook, stirring constantly, until the sauce thickens and becomes translucent. Remove from the heat and pour the sauce over the fish. Stir carefully around the fish and return the frying-pan to moderate heat. Cook, turning the pieces occasionally, for 2 minutes.

Transfer the mixture to a warmed serving dish and serve at once.

Serves 4

Preparation and cooking time: 30 minutes

Kuo Tieh Yu Pien

(Egg-Braised Sliced Fish)

Whiting or plaice (flounder) fillets can be used instead of sole, if you wish to economize in this recipe.

Metric/Imperial	American
½kg./1lb. sole fillets, cut into small strips about 5cm./2in. x 2.5cm./1in.	1lb. sole fillets, cut into small strips about 2in. x 1in.
2½ tsp. salt	2½ tsp. salt
2.5cm./1in. piece of fresh root ginger, peeled and grated	1in. piece of fresh green ginger, peeled and grated
1½ Tbs. cornflour	1½ Tbs. cornstarch
1 Tbs. corn oil	1 Tbs. corn oil
3 eggs, lightly beaten	3 eggs, lightly beaten
vegetable oil for deep-frying	vegetable oil for deep-frying
75ml./3fl.oz. sesame oil	⅓ cup sesame oil
50ml./2fl.oz. chicken stock	¼ cup chicken stock
2 Tbs. rice wine or dry sherry	2 Tbs. rice wine or dry sherry
1 Tbs. chopped parsley	1 Tbs. chopped parsley
1½ Tbs. soya sauce	1½ Tbs. soy sauce
1½ Tbs. lemon juice	1½ Tbs. lemon juice

Sprinkle the fish strips with 1½ teaspoons of salt, the ginger, cornflour (cornstarch) and corn oil, rubbing them into the flesh with your fingers. Set aside for 1 hour. Beat the eggs and remaining salt together, and set aside.

Fill a large saucepan one-third full with oil and heat until it is very hot. Carefully lower the fish strips into the oil, a few at a time, and fry for 1½ minutes, or until they are lightly browned and crisp. Remove from the oil and drain on kitchen towels.

Heat the sesame oil in a large frying-pan. When it is hot, add the fish strips, in one layer if possible, and fry for 1 minute. Pour in the beaten egg, tilting the pan so that the oil flows freely and the fish strips move and slide in the pan. When the egg is half-set, remove the pan from the heat and turn the fish strips over. Return the pan to the heat. When the egg has completely set, sprinkle over the stock and wine or sherry. Turn the fish strips over once more and cook for a further 30 seconds.

Transfer the strips to a warmed served dish, arranging them in one layer. Sprinkle over the remaining ingredients, and serve at once.

Serves 4-6

Preparation and cooking time: 1½ hours

Hwang chi yu Pien

(Sliced Fish in Tomato Sauce)

Metric/Imperial	American
½kg./1lb. lemon sole fillets, skinned	1lb. lemon sole fillets, skinned
1 tsp. salt	1 tsp. salt
¼ tsp. ground ginger	¼ tsp. ground ginger
1 Tbs. cornflour	1 Tbs. cornstarch
1 egg white, lightly beaten	1 egg white, lightly beaten
75ml./3fl.oz. vegetable oil	⅓ cup vegetable oil
SAUCE	SAUCE
20g./¾oz. butter	1½ Tbs. butter
4 medium tomatoes, blanched, peeled and quartered	4 medium tomatoes, blanched, peeled and quartered
2½ Tbs. soya sauce	2½ Tbs. soy sauce
2 Tbs. tomato purée	2 Tbs. tomato paste
2 tsp. cornflour	2 tsp. cornstarch
75ml./3fl.oz. chicken stock	⅓ cup chicken stock
2 Tbs. sherry	2 Tbs. sherry

Cut the sole fillets into 5cm./2in. by 2.5cm./1in. slices. Mix the salt, ginger and cornflour (cornstarch) together in a shallow dish. Add the fish pieces and coat them thoroughly. Mix in the egg white, and toss gently until the pieces are coated.

Heat the oil in a large frying-pan. When it is hot, remove the pan from the heat and carefully slide the fish pieces, well spaced, into the pan. Return to the heat and cook the fish for 1 minute, tilting the pan from side to side so that the oil flows around. Turn over and cook for 30 seconds. Remove from the heat and transfer the fish to a plate. Cover and keep hot.

Pour off the oil from the pan and return to the heat. Add the butter and melt it. Add the tomato quarters to the pan and cook for 2 minutes, stirring constantly. Stir in the soy sauce and tomato purée (paste) and cook for 30 seconds.

Combine the cornflour (cornstarch), stock, wine or sherry and sugar and pour into the pan. Cook, stirring constantly, until the sauce thickens and becomes translucent. Return the fish to the pan and coat them gently in the sauce. Reduce the heat to low and simmer for 2 minutes.

Transfer the mixture to a warmed serving dish and serve at once.

Serves 4

Preparation and cooking time: 25 minutes

Chinese Steamed Fish

Metric/Imperial	American
2 firm white fish fillets or small steaks	2 firm white fish fillets or small steaks
125g./4oz. button mushrooms, thinly sliced	1 cup thinly sliced button mushrooms
1 tsp. cornflour	1 tsp. cornstarch
2 Tbs. soya sauce	2 Tbs. soy sauce
2 spring onions, finely chopped	2 scallions, finely chopped
1 garlic clove, crushed	1 garlic clove, crushed
4 Tbs. sesame oil	4 Tbs. sesame oil
1 Tbs. white wine vinegar	1 Tbs. white wine vinegar
$\frac{1}{4}$ tsp. sugar	$\frac{1}{4}$ tsp. sugar
salt and pepper	salt and pepper

Bamboo steamers, universally popular in China, are filled with fish and placed on a steamer shelf over a wok – this is a very successful method of cooking as it retains the flavour and goodness of the fish.

Arrange the fish pieces on a large lightly greased heatproof plate. Scatter over the mushrooms and set aside.

Combine the cornflour (cornstarch) and soy sauce until they are well blended, then gradually stir in all of the remaining ingredients. Pour the mixture over the fish. Cover with foil or a second heatproof plate, and arrange in the top half of a steamer. Half-fill the bottom half of the steamer with boiling water, set the pan over moderately low heat and steam the fish for 10 to 15 minutes, or until the flesh flakes easily.

Remove from the heat and transfer the fish and sauce mixture to a warmed serving dish. Serve at once.

Serves 2
Preparation and cooking time: 25 minutes

Pao Yu Ts'Ai Hsin

(Stir-Fried Abalone and Chinese Cabbage)

Metric/Imperial	American
3 Tbs. peanut oil	3 Tbs. peanut oil
2.5cm./1in. piece of fresh root ginger, peeled and chopped	1in. piece of fresh green ginger, peeled and chopped
1 small leek, white part only, thinly sliced into rings	1 small leek, white part only, thinly sliced into rings
1 small Chinese cabbage, shredded	1 small Chinese cabbage, shredded
$\frac{1}{4}$ tsp. monosodium glutamate (optional)	$\frac{1}{4}$ tsp. MSG (optional)
salt and white pepper to taste	salt and white pepper to taste
2 tsp. soya sauce	2 tsp. soy sauce
$1\frac{1}{2}$ Tbs. fresh lemon juice	$1\frac{1}{2}$ Tbs. fresh lemon juice
450g./1lb. tinned abalone, drained and sliced	1lb. canned abalone, drained and sliced

Pao Tu Ts'Ai Hsin contains Chinese cabbage and abalone, a shellfish famous for its yield of high-grade mother-of-pearl.

Heat the oil in a large frying-pan. When it is hot, add the ginger and leek and stir-fry for 2 minutes. Add the cabbage and stir-fry for 4 minutes, or until the cabbage is cooked but still crisp. Sprinkle over the monosodium glutamate (MSG), if you are using it, salt, pepper, soy sauce and lemon juice. Stir in the abalone and cook for 5 minutes, stirring constantly.

Transfer the mixture to a warmed serving dish and serve at once.

Serves 4-6

Preparation and cooking time: 25 minutes

Steamed Bass with Black Bean Sauce

Fermented black beans can be purchased from Chinese or oriental delicatessens.

Metric/Imperial	American
1 x 1kg./2lb. sea bass, gutted (the head and tail can be left on or removed, as you wish)	1 x 2lb. sea bass, gutted (the head and tail can be left on or removed, as you wish)
125ml./4fl.oz. rice wine or dry sherry	½ cup rice wine or dry sherry
5cm./2in. piece of fresh root ginger, peeled and chopped	2in. piece of fresh green ginger, peeled and chopped
SAUCE	SAUCE
3 Tbs. vegetable oil	3 Tbs. vegetable oil
5cm./2in. piece of fresh root ginger, peeled and chopped	2in. piece of fresh green ginger, peeled and chopped
2 spring onions, chopped	2 scallions, chopped
2 garlic cloves, crushed	2 garlic cloves, crushed
2 tsp. sugar	2 tsp. sugar
2 Tbs. fermented black beans	2 Tbs. fermented black beans
2 Tbs. soya sauce	2 Tbs. soy sauce
2 Tbs. rice wine or dry sherry	2 Tbs. rice wine or dry sherry

Arrange the fish on a heatproof dish and pour over the wine or sherry. Scatter over the chopped ginger. Half-fill the bottom half of a double boiler or steamer with water and bring to the boil. Put the dish into the top half and arrange over the boiling water. Cover and steam over moderate heat for 20 to 25 minutes, or until the fish flakes easily.

Meanwhile, to make the sauce, heat the oil in a frying-pan. When it is hot, add the ginger, spring onions (scallions), and garlic and stir-fry for 2 minutes. Add all the remaining ingredients and bring to the boil, stirring constantly. Cook for 1 minute.

Remove the fish from the steamer and transfer to a warmed serving dish. Pour over the sauce and serve at once.

Serves 4-6
Preparation and cooking time: 35 minutes

Abalone with Mushrooms in Oyster Sauce

Metric/Imperial	American
3 Tbs. vegetable oil	3 Tbs. vegetable oil
8 dried mushrooms, soaked in cold water for 30 minutes, drained and sliced	8 dried mushrooms, soaked in cold water for 30 minutes, drained and sliced
2 spring onions, chopped	2 scallions, chopped
4 Tbs. rice wine or dry sherry	4 Tbs. rice wine or dry sherry
125ml./4fl.oz. oyster sauce	½ cup oyster sauce
½ tsp. soft brown sugar	½ tsp. soft brown sugar
2 tsp. cornflour, mixed to a paste with 2 Tbs. water	2 tsp. cornstarch, mixed to a paste with 2 Tbs. water
450g./1lb. tinned abalone, drained and sliced	1lb. canned abalone, drained and sliced

Heat the oil in a large frying-pan. When it is hot, add the mushrooms and spring onions (scallions) and stir-fry for 2 minutes. Stir in the wine or sherry, oyster sauce and sugar and bring to the boil. Add the abalone slices and baste well. Cook for 5 minutes, turning occasionally, or until the abalone is heated through.

Transfer the abalone slices to a warmed serving dish and keep hot. Stir the cornflour (cornstarch) mixture into the pan and cook, stirring constantly, until the sauce thickens and becomes translucent. Pour over the abalone slices and serve at once.

Serves 4-6
Preparation and cooking time: 30 minutes

Velvet Crab

Metric/Imperial	American
300ml./10fl.oz. single cream	1¼ cups light cream
250ml./8fl.oz. water	1 cup water
1 tsp. sugar	1 tsp. sugar
½ tsp. salt	½ tsp. salt
½ tsp. white pepper	½ tsp. white pepper
3 eggs, lightly beaten	3 eggs, lightly beaten
1 Tbs. cornflour, mixed to a paste with 2 Tbs. water	1 Tbs. cornstarch, mixed to a paste with 2 Tbs. water
1 tsp. paprika	1 tsp. paprika
350g./12oz. crabmeat, shell and cartilage removed and flaked	12oz. crabmeat, shell and cartilage removed and flaked
225g./8oz. vermicelli, deep-fried until crisp, drained and kept hot	8oz. vermicelli, deep-fried until crisp, drained and kept hot

Put the cream, water, sugar, salt and pepper into a large saucepan and bring to the boil. Reduce the heat to low and, using a wire whisk or beater, beat in the eggs. Stir in the cornflour (cornstarch) mixture and paprika and beat until smooth and thick. Stir in the crabmeat and cook for 2 minutes, or until the crabmeat is heated through. Remove from the heat.

Arrange the vermicelli on a warmed serving dish and spoon over the crabmeat mixture. Serve at once.

Serves 4
Preparation and cooking time: 25 minutes

Shrimps Stir-Fried with Ginger

Metric/Imperial	American
2 Tbs. vegetable oil	2 Tbs. vegetable oil
3 garlic cloves, crushed	3 garlic cloves, crushed
2 spring onions, chopped	2 scallions, chopped
1 leek, white part only, cut into thin strips	1 leek, white part only, cut into thin strips
7.5cm./3in. piece of fresh root ginger, peeled and finely chopped	3in. piece of fresh green ginger, peeled and finely chopped
2 Tbs. soya sauce	2 Tbs. soy sauce
1 tsp. sugar	1 tsp. sugar

¼ tsp. salt
700g./1½lb. frozen peeled shrimps,
    thawed and drained
225g./8oz. bean sprouts
125g./4oz. petits pois

¼ tsp. salt
1½lb. frozen peeled shrimp, thawed and
    drained
1 cup bean sprouts
½ cup petits pois

Heat the oil in a frying-pan. When it is hot, add the garlic, spring onions (scallions), leek and ginger and stir-fry for 3 minutes. Add the soy sauce, sugar and salt and stir-fry for 1 minute.

    Stir in the shrimps, bean sprouts and petits pois and stir-fry for 5 minutes. Transfer to a warmed serving dish and serve.

Serves 4
Preparation and cooking time: 20 minutes

Velvet Crab, as its name suggests, is an elegant dish of crabmeat and cream, served on a crisp layer of vermicelli.

This recipe for crispy Prawn or Shrimp Fritters served with a savoury dip is delicious as an hors d'oeuvre or as a light meal.

Prawn or Shrimp Fritters

Metric/Imperial	American
700g./1½lb. prawns, shelled, with the tails left on and deveined	1½lb. shrimp, peeled, with the tails left on and deveined
6 Tbs. cornflour	6 Tbs. cornstarch
1 tsp. salt	1 tsp. salt
¼ tsp. cayenne pepper	¼ tsp. cayenne pepper
2 eggs, separated	2 eggs, separated
3 Tbs. water	3 Tbs. water
vegetable oil for deep-frying	vegetable oil for deep-frying
SAUCE	SAUCE
1 Tbs. wine vinegar	1 Tbs. wine vinegar
1 Tbs. soft brown sugar	1 Tbs. soft brown sugar
1 Tbs. tomato purée	1 Tbs. tomato paste
1 Tbs. soya sauce	1 Tbs. soy sauce
1 Tbs. vegetable oil	1 Tbs. vegetable oil
¼ tsp. salt	¼ tsp. salt
50ml./2fl.oz. rice wine or dry sherry	¼ cup rice wine or dry sherry
1 Tbs. cornflour, mixed to a paste with 125ml./4fl.oz. water	1 Tbs. cornstarch, mixed to a paste with ½ cup water
2 lemons, cut into wedges	2 lemons, cut into wedges

Wash the prawns (shrimp) in cold water and drain on kitchen towels.

Combine the cornflour (cornstarch), salt and cayenne. Make a well in the centre and add the egg yolks and water. Slowly incorporate the dry ingredients into the liquids until the mixture forms a smooth batter. Set aside for 20 minutes.

Meanwhile, make the sauce. Put the ingredients, except the cornflour (cornstarch) mixture, into a saucepan and bring to the boil, stirring constantly. Reduce the heat to low and stir in the cornflour (cornstarch) mixture. Cook, stirring constantly, until the sauce thickens and becomes translucent. Remove from the heat and set aside.

Beat the egg whites until they form stiff peaks, fold into the egg yolk batter.

Fill a large saucepan one-third full with oil and heat until it is hot. Holding the prawns (shrimp) by the tails, dip each one in the batter then drop them carefully into the oil, a few at a time. Fry for 3 to 4 minutes, or until they are golden brown. Remove from the oil and drain on kitchen towels.

Arrange the fritters on a warmed serving dish and garnish with the lemon wedges. Reheat the sauce, then pour into small individual bowls. Serve at once, with the fritters.

Serves 6-8
Preparation and cooking time: 1 hour

Cantonese Lobster

Metric/Imperial	American
1 x 1kg./2lb. lobster, claws cracked and sac removed	1 x 2lb. lobster, claws cracked and sac removed
75ml./3fl.oz. peanut oil	$\frac{1}{3}$ cup peanut oil
1 garlic clove, crushed	1 garlic clove, crushed
5cm./2in. piece of fresh root ginger, peeled and chopped	2in. piece of fresh green ginger, peeled and chopped
125g./4oz. lean pork, minced	4oz. lean pork, ground
250ml./8fl.oz. chicken stock	1 cup chicken stock
1 Tbs. rice wine or dry sherry	1 Tbs. rice wine or dry sherry
1 Tbs. soya sauce	1 Tbs. soy sauce
1 tsp. sugar	1 tsp. sugar
1 Tbs. cornflour, mixed to a paste with 2 Tbs. water	1 Tbs. cornstarch, mixed to a paste with 2 Tbs. water
3 spring onions, chopped	3 scallions, chopped
2 eggs	2 eggs

Cut the lobster into bite-sized pieces and set aside.

Heat half the oil in a large, deep frying-pan. When it is hot, add the garlic and stir-fry for 1 minute. Add the lobster pieces and stir-fry for 3 to 5 minutes, or until they are heated through. Transfer to a warmed serving dish and keep hot while you cook the sauce.

Heat the remaining oil in the same frying-pan. When it is hot, add the ginger and pork and fry, stirring constantly, until the pork loses its pinkness. Pour over the stock and bring to the boil, stirring constantly. Combine the wine or sherry, soy sauce and sugar, then stir the mixture into the pan. Stir-fry for 1 minute. Stir in the cornflour (cornstarch) mixture and cook, stirring constantly, until the sauce thickens and becomes translucent. Stir in the spring onions (scallions) and stir-fry for 1 minute.

Turn off the heat and beat the eggs once or twice until they are just combined. Gently pour them over the pan mixture, lifting the sides of the mixture to allow the egg to run over and under. When the eggs become creamy and slightly 'set', spoon the sauce over the lobster and serve at once.

Serves 2-4
Preparation and cooking time: 40 minutes

Shrimps with Eggs and Petits-pois

Metric/Imperial	American
5 eggs	5 eggs
1 tsp. salt	1 tsp. salt
25g./1oz. butter	2 Tbs. butter
2.5cm./1in. piece of fresh root ginger, peeled and chopped	1in. piece of fresh green ginger, peeled and chopped
1 small onion, sliced	1 small onion, sliced
125g./4oz. small shelled shrimps	4oz. small peeled shrimp
225g./8oz. petits pois	1 cup petits pois
1 Tbs. soya sauce	1 Tbs. soy sauce
½ tsp. sugar	½ tsp. sugar
2 Tbs. vegetable oil	2 Tbs. vegetable oil

Beat the eggs and salt together until they are blended. Set aside.

Melt the butter in a saucepan. Add the ginger and onion and stir-fry for 30 seconds. Add the shrimps, petits pois, soy sauce and sugar and stir-fry for a further 1½ minutes. Remove from the heat and set aside.

Heat the oil in a large frying-pan. When it is hot, pour in the egg mixture. Stir, then leave for a few seconds until the bottom sets. Remove from the heat and add the shrimps and petits pois. Turn, mix and toss the mixture a few times. Return to the heat and cook for 1 minute, stirring occasionally.

Transfer the mixture to a warmed serving dish and serve at once.
Serves 2-3
Preparation and cooking time: 20 minutes

Quick Fried Shrimps with Cashews

Metric/Imperial	American
½kg./1lb. small shelled shrimps	1lb. small peeled shrimp
1 Tbs. rice wine or sherry	1 Tbs. rice wine or sherry
1 egg white, lightly beaten	1 egg white, lightly beaten
1½ Tbs. cornflour	1½ Tbs. cornstarch
salt and pepper	salt and pepper
1 tsp. ground ginger	1 tsp. ground ginger
50ml./2fl.oz. vegetable oil	¼ cup vegetable oil
125g./4oz. unsalted cashews	1 cup unsalted cashews
5cm./2in. piece of fresh root ginger, peeled and chopped	2in. piece of fresh root ginger, peeled and chopped
3 spring onions, chopped	3 scallions, chopped

Put the shrimps into a shallow dish. Beat half the wine or sherry, the egg white, 1 tablespoon of cornflour (cornstarch), seasoning and ground ginger together until the mixture forms a smooth batter. Pour over the shrimps and toss gently to coat them. Set aside for 30 minutes.

Heat the oil in a large, deep-frying-pan. When it is hot, add the cashews and fry, turning occasionally, for 5 minutes. Push them to the side of the pan and stir in the shrimps. Stir-fry for 3 minutes, or until they are heated through. Stir in the remaining ingredients, except the wine or sherry and cornflour (cornstarch) and stir-fry for a further 2 minutes. Stir in the remaining wine or sherry and cornflour (cornstarch) and mix the cashews into the other ingredients. Cook, stirring constantly, until the sauce thickens and becomes translucent.

Transfer the mixture to a warmed serving dish and serve at once.
Serves 6
Preparation and cooking time: 25 minutes

Stir-Fry Shrimps with Mange-tout

Metric/Imperial	American
3 Tbs. vegetable oil	3 Tbs. vegetable oil
350g./12oz. shelled shrimps	2 cups peeled shrimp
225g./8oz. mange-tout, cut into 5cm./2in. lengths	1⅓ cups snow peas, cut into 2in. lengths
125g./4oz. bean sprouts	½ cup bean sprouts
2 Tbs. rice wine or dry sherry	2 Tbs. rice wine or dry sherry
1 Tbs. soya sauce	1 Tbs. soy sauce
½ tsp. soft brown sugar	½ tsp. soft brown sugar
1 Tbs. cornflour, mixed to a paste with 2 Tbs. water	1 Tbs. cornstarch, mixed to a paste with 2 Tbs. water

Heat the oil in a large frying-pan. When it is hot, add the shrimps and stir-fry for 2 minutes. Add the mange-tout (snow peas) and bean sprouts and stir-fry for a further 2 minutes. Add all the remaining ingredients and bring to the boil, stirring constantly. Cook, stirring constantly, until the sauce thickens and becomes translucent.

Transfer the mixture to a warmed serving dish and serve at once.
Serves 4
Preparation and cooking time: 20 minutes

Hwang Chi Hsia Ren

(Shrimps in Tomato Sauce)

Metric/Imperial	American
½kg./1lb. shrimps, shelled	1lb. shrimp, peeled
1 tsp. salt	1 tsp. salt
½ tsp. ground ginger	½ tsp. ground ginger
1½ tsp. cornflour	1½ tsp. cornstarch
75ml./3fl.oz. vegetable oil	⅓ cup vegetable oil
SAUCE	SAUCE
20g./¾oz. butter	1½ Tbs. butter
3 medium tomatoes, blanched, peeled and quartered	3 medium tomatoes, blanched, peeled and quartered
2½ Tbs. soya sauce	2½ Tbs. soy sauce
2 Tbs. tomato purée	2 Tbs. tomato paste
2 tsp. cornflour	2 tsp. cornstarch
75ml./3fl.oz. chicken stock	⅓ cup chicken stock
2 Tbs. rice wine or sherry	2 Tbs. rice wine or sherry
1 tsp. sugar	1 tsp. sugar

Put the shrimps in a shallow dish. Sprinkle over the salt, ginger and cornflour (cornstarch) and rub them in to the flesh with your fingers.

Heat the oil in a large frying-pan. When it is hot, add the shrimps and fry for 2 minutes, stirring constantly. Remove from the heat and, using a slotted spoon, transfer the shrimps to a plate. Cover and keep hot.

Pour off the oil from the pan and return to the heat. Add the butter and melt it. When it has melted, add the tomato quarters and fry for 2 minutes, stirring constantly. Stir in the soy sauce and tomato purée (paste) and cook for a further 30 seconds.

Combine the cornflour (cornstarch), stock, wine or sherry and sugar. Pour the mixture into the pan and cook, stirring constantly, until the sauce thickens and becomes translucent. Return the shrimps to the sauce and baste well. Cook for a further 1½ minutes, stirring constantly.

Transfer the mixture to a warmed serving dish and serve at once.

Serves 4
Preparation and cooking time: 25 minutes

Shrimps with Bean Curd

Metric/Imperial	American
½kg./1lb. shelled shrimps	1lb. peeled shrimp
1 tsp. salt	1 tsp. salt
½ tsp. ground ginger	½ tsp. ground ginger
2 Tbs. cornflour	2 Tbs. cornstarch
50ml./2fl.oz. vegetable oil	4 Tbs. vegetable oil
10cm./4in. piece of fresh root ginger, peeled and chopped	4in. piece of fresh green ginger, peeled and chopped
1 garlic clove, crushed	1 garlic clove, crushed
1 dried red chilli, chopped	1 dried red chilli, chopped
3 bean curd cakes, sliced then chopped	3 bean curd cakes, sliced then chopped
50ml./2fl.oz. chicken stock	¼ cup chicken stock
2 Tbs. water	2 Tbs. water

Put the shrimps into a shallow dish. Sprinkle over the salt, ground ginger and half the cornflour (cornstarch) and gently rub them into the flesh with your fingers. Set aside for 10 minutes.

Heat the oil in a large, deep frying-pan. When it is hot, add the ginger and garlic and stir-fry for 1 minute. Add the chilli and stir-fry for 30 seconds. Stir in the bean curd and stock, reduce the heat to low and simmer for 3 minutes, stirring occasionally.

Mix the remaining cornflour (cornstarch) with the water, then stir into the pan mixture. Cook, stirring constantly, until the sauce thickens.

Transfer the mixture to a warmed serving dish and serve at once.
Serves 4-6
Preparation and cooking time: 25 minutes

Winter Prawns or Shrimps

Metric/Imperial	American
10 egg whites	10 egg whites
2 tsp. cornflour	2 tsp. cornstarch
½ tsp. salt	½ tsp. salt

175g./6oz. prawns	1 cup peeled shrimp
vegetable oil for deep-frying	vegetable oil for deep-frying
¼ tsp. monosodium glutamate (optional)	¼ tsp. MSG (optional)
50g./2oz. cooked chicken, minced	¼ cup ground cooked chicken
2 Tbs. chopped chives	2 Tbs. chopped chives

Winter Prawns will form a fairy-light and exquisite part of any Chinese dinner.

Beat 1 egg white, the cornflour (cornstarch) and salt together until they form a smooth batter. Put the prawns (shrimp) in the batter and gently toss to coat thoroughly.

Fill a large saucepan one-third full with oil and heat until it is very hot. Arrange the prawns (shrimp) in a deep-frying basket and carefully lower into the oil. Fry for 1 minute. Remove from the oil and drain on kitchen towels. Set aside.

Beat the remaining egg whites with the monosodium glutamate (MSG). Pile half the egg whites on to a dish. Lay the prawns (shrimp) on top and, using a spatula, gently spread the remaining egg whites over the top. Carefully tilt the pan over the saucepan containing the oil and gently slide it into the oil. Fry for 3 minutes basting the top with oil if it is not fully covered. Remove the pan from the heat and, using a fish slice or spatula, remove from the oil and drain on kitchen towels.

Transfer the mixture to a warmed serving dish and sprinkle over the chicken and chives. Serve at once.
Serves 4-6
Preparation and cooking time: 30 minutes

Prawn Balls with Green Peas

Metric/Imperial	American
50g./2oz. cornflour	½ cup cornstarch
vegetable oil for deep-frying	vegetable oil for deep-frying
2 Tbs. peanut oil	2 Tbs. peanut oil

Metric/Imperial	American
4cm./1½in. piece of fresh root ginger, peeled and finely chopped	1½in. piece of fresh green ginger, peeled and finely chopped
1 Tbs. wine vinegar	1 Tbs. wine vinegar
1 Tbs. soya sauce	1 Tbs. soy sauce
1 Tbs. tomato purée	1 Tbs. tomato paste
2 tsp. soft brown sugar	2 tsp. soft brown sugar
125ml./4fl.oz. chicken stock	½ cup chicken stock
125g./4oz. frozen green peas, thawed	½ cup frozen green peas, thawed
1 Tbs. cornflour, blended to a paste with 1½ Tbs. water	1 Tbs. cornstarch mixed to a paste with 1½ Tbs. water
PRAWN BALLS	PRAWN BALLS
½kg./1lb. shelled prawns, finely chopped	1lb. peeled shrimp, finely chopped
1 tsp. ground ginger	1 tsp. ground ginger
2 Tbs. fresh white breadcrumbs	2 Tbs. fresh white breadcrumbs
1 tsp. cornflour	1 tsp. cornstarch
1 egg yolk	1 egg yolk

First make the prawn (shrimp) balls. Combine all the ingredients in a mixing bowl. Using your hands, shape the mixture into small, walnut-sized balls. Toss gently in the cornflour (cornstarch).

Fill a large saucepan about one-third full with vegetable oil and heat it until it is very hot. Carefully lower the prawn (shrimp) balls, a few at a time, into the hot oil and fry until they are golden brown and crisp. Remove from the oil and drain on kitchen towels. Set aside.

Heat the peanut oil in a large frying-pan. When it is hot, add the ginger and stir-fry for 1 minute. Add the vinegar, soy sauce, tomato purée (paste), sugar and stock and stir until they are well blended. Stir in the peas and bring to the boil. Return the prawn (shrimp) balls to the pan and stir-fry for 2 minutes.

Stir in the cornflour (cornstarch) mixture and cook until the sauce thickens and becomes translucent. Transfer the mixture to a warmed serving dish and serve at once.

Serves 4-6
Preparation and cooking time: 30 minutes

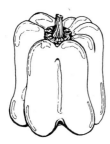

Prawns or Shrimps in Sweet and Sour Sauce

Metric/Imperial	American
3 Tbs. vegetable oil	3 Tbs. vegetable oil
700g./1½lb. Dublin Bay prawns, shelled	1½ lb. large Gulf shrimp, peeled
¼ tsp. cayenne pepper	¼ tsp. cayenne pepper
SAUCE	SAUCE
2 tsp. soya sauce	2 tsp. soy sauce
2 Tbs. soft brown sugar	2 Tbs. soft brown sugar
2 Tbs. vegetable oil	2 Tbs. vegetable oil
2 Tbs. wine vinegar	2 Tbs. wine vinegar
½ tsp. ground ginger	½ tsp. ground ginger
salt and pepper to taste	salt and pepper to taste
300ml./10fl.oz. pineapple juice	1¼ cups pineapple juice
1 large green pepper, pith and seeds removed and cut into 1cm./½in. lengths	1 large green pepper, pith and seeds removed and cut into ½in. lengths
2 Tbs. cornflour, mixed to a paste with 6 Tbs. water	2 Tbs. cornstarch, mixed to a paste with 6 Tbs. water

Heat the oil in a large frying-pan. When it is hot, add the prawns (shrimp) and sprinkle over the cayenne. Cook for 5 minutes, stirring frequently.

Meanwhile, to make the sauce put the ingredients, except the pepper and corn-flour (cornstarch) mixture, into a saucepan and bring to the boil, stirring constantly. Add the pepper, reduce the heat to low and cover the pan. Simmer for 3 minutes. Stir in the cornflour (cornstarch) mixture. Cook, stirring constantly, until the sauce thickens and becomes translucent. Remove from the heat.

Arrange the prawns (shrimp) on a warmed serving dish and pour over the sauce. Serve at once.

Serves 6
Preparation and cooking time: 20 minutes

A splash of colour on a bed of fried rice, Prawns or Shrimps in Sweet and Sour Sauce make a tempting main dish.

VEGETABLES

Chow Barg Choy

(Fried Cabbage)

Metric/Imperial	American
2 Tbs. vegetable oil	2 Tbs. vegetable oil
1 garlic clove, crushed	1 garlic clove, crushed
700g./1½lb. Chinese cabbage, shredded	3½ cups shredded Chinese cabbage
½ tsp. salt	½ tsp. salt
75ml./3fl.oz. water	⅓ cup water
2 tsp. soya sauce	2 tsp. soy sauce
1 tsp. flour	1 tsp. flour
½ tsp. sugar	½ tsp. sugar

Heat the oil in a large, deep frying-pan. When it is hot, add the garlic and stir-fry for 1 minute. Add the cabbage and salt and cook for 6 minutes, stirring occasionally.

Combine the water, soy sauce and flour together until they form a smooth paste. Stir in the sugar, then pour the mixture into the pan. Stir-fry for 2 minutes.

Remove the pan from the heat and transfer the mixture to a warmed serving bowl. Serve at once.

Serves 4-6
Preparation and cooking time: 25 minutes

Nai-Yu-Ts'Ai Hsin

(Cabbage in Cream Sauce)

Metric/Imperial	American
15g./½oz. butter	1 Tbs. butter
1 Tbs. sesame oil	1 Tbs. sesame oil
3 spring onions, sliced	3 scallions, sliced
2 small Chinese cabbages, shredded	2 small Chinese cabbages, shredded
salt and pepper	salt and pepper
1 Tbs. white wine vinegar	1 Tbs. white wine vinegar
125ml./4fl.oz. single cream	½ cup light cream
2 tsp. soya sauce	2 tsp. soy sauce

Melt the butter with the oil in a large frying-pan. When it is hot, add the spring onions (scallions) and cabbage and stir-fry for 3 minutes. Sprinkle over the salt, pepper and vinegar and stir-fry for a further 3 minutes, or until the cabbage is cooked but still crisp.

Stir in the remaining ingredients and cook, stirring frequently, for 4 minutes, or until the sauce comes to the boil. Transfer the mixture to a warmed serving dish and serve at once.

Serves 6-8
Preparation and cooking time: 25 minutes

A *savoury recipe for cab-bage, Hung Shao Pai Ts'Ai, through being cook-ed only for a very short time, remains delectably crunchy.*

Hung Shao Pai Ts'Ai

(Red-Cooked Cabbage)

Metric/Imperial	American
40g./1½oz. butter	3 Tbs. butter
3 Tbs. vegetable oil	3 Tbs. vegetable oil
1 Chinese cabbage, shredded	1 Chinese cabbage, shredded
3½ tsp. sugar	3½ tsp. sugar
5 Tbs. soya sauce	5 Tbs. soy sauce
3 Tbs. water	3 Tbs. water
½ chicken stock cube, crumbled	½ chicken bouillon cube, crumbled
3 Tbs. rice wine or dry sherry	3 Tbs. rice wine or dry sherry

Melt the butter with the oil in a large frying-pan. When it is hot, add the cabbage and turn it in the mixture until thoroughly coated. Reduce the heat to low, cover and simmer for 5 minutes. Stir in the sugar, soy sauce, water, stock (bouillon) cube, wine and sherry and simmer, covered, for a further 5 minutes.

Transfer the mixture to a warmed serving dish and serve at once.

Serves 6

Preparation and cooking time: 20 minutes

Bamboo Shoot with Mushrooms

Metric/Imperial	American
350g./12oz. bamboo shoot, thinly sliced	2 cups thinly sliced bamboo shoot
50ml./2fl.oz. peanut oil	¼ cup peanut oil
10 dried mushrooms, soaked in cold water for 30 minutes, drained and sliced	10 dried mushrooms, soaked in cold water for 30 minutes, drained and sliced
2 Tbs. rice wine or dry sherry	2 Tbs. rice wine or dry sherry
4 Tbs. soya sauce	4 Tbs. soy sauce
1 Tbs. sugar	1 Tbs. sugar
75ml./3fl.oz. water	⅓ cup water
½ Tbs. cornflour, mixed to a paste with 2 Tbs. water	½ Tbs. cornstarch, mixed to a paste with 2 Tbs. water

Bean Curd, cakes of cooked, puréed soya beans and seen here with Bean Curd Skin (strips of dried curd), is one of the most important products made from the soya bean. It is used extensively throughout the Orient.

Heat a large frying-pan over moderate heat for 30 seconds. Add the oil and swirl it around the pan. Add the bamboo shoots and mushrooms and fry for 5 minutes, stirring frequently.

Stir in all the remaining ingredients and bring to the boil, stirring constantly. Cook, stirring constantly, until the sauce thickens and becomes translucent.

Transfer the mixture to a warmed serving dish and serve at once.

Serves 4

Preparation and cooking time: 30 minutes

Bean Curd with Spiced Meat and Vegetables

Metric/Imperial	American
50ml./2fl.oz. peanut oil	¼ cup peanut oil
1 garlic clove, crushed	1 garlic clove, crushed
7½cm./3in. piece of fresh root ginger, peeled and chopped	3in. piece of fresh green ginger, peeled and chopped
4 spring onions, chopped	4 scallions, chopped
4 dried mushrooms, soaked in cold water for 30 minutes, drained and chopped	4 dried mushrooms, soaked in cold water for 30 minutes, drained and chopped
1 tsp. red pepper flakes	1 tsp. red pepper flakes
2 dried chillis, chopped	2 dried chillis, chopped
175g./6oz. minced beef	6oz. ground beef
2 Tbs. soya sauce	2 Tbs. soy sauce
250ml./8fl.oz. chicken stock	1 cup chicken stock
3 bean curd cakes, mashed	3 bean curd cakes, mashed
1 Tbs. cornflour, mixed to a paste with 2 Tbs. stock	1 Tbs. cornstarch, mixed to a paste with 2 Tbs. stock

Heat the oil in a large saucepan. When it is hot, add the garlic, ginger, spring onions (scallions) and mushrooms and stir-fry for 3 minutes. Stir in the red pepper flakes and chillis and stir-fry for a further 1 minute. Add the minced (ground) meat and fry until it loses its pinkness. Pour over the soy sauce and stock and bring to the boil, stirring constantly.

Stir in the bean curd and stir-fry for 3 minutes. Add the cornflour (cornstarch) mixture and cook, stirring constantly, until the sauce thickens.

Transfer the mixture to a warmed serving dish and serve at once.

Serves 6
Preparation and cooking time: 30 minutes

Stir-Fried Mixed Vegetables with Egg

Metric/Imperial	American
3 Tbs. peanut oil	3 Tbs. peanut oil
5cm./2in. piece of fresh root ginger, peeled and chopped	2in. piece of fresh green ginger, peeled and chopped
5 spring onions, chopped	5 scallions, chopped
125g./4oz. mushrooms, sliced	1 cup sliced mushrooms
125g./4oz. bean sprouts	½ cup bean sprouts
salt and pepper to taste	salt and pepper to taste
1½ Tbs. soya sauce	1½ Tbs. soy sauce
3 eggs, lightly beaten	3 eggs, lightly beaten

Heat the oil in a large frying-pan. When it is hot, add the ginger and stir-fry for 1 minute. Add the spring onions (scallions) and mushrooms and stir-fry for 2 minutes. Stir in the bean sprouts, seasoning and soy sauce and stir-fry for a further 2 minutes.

Pour over the eggs, stir them with a fork and leave for a few seconds to allow the bottom to set. Stir again with the fork and leave until the eggs are creamy.

Transfer the mixture to a warmed serving dish and serve at once.

Serves 4
Preparation and cooking time: 20 minutes

Stir-Fried Mixed Vegetables

Metric/Imperial	American
4 Tbs. sesame oil	4 Tbs. sesame oil
4cm./1½in. piece of fresh root ginger, peeled and chopped	1½in. piece of fresh green ginger, peeled and chopped
1 large leek, cleaned and cut into 2.5cm./1in. lengths	1 large leek, cleaned and cut into 1in. lengths
2 large carrots, thinly sliced	2 large carrots, thinly sliced
1 large red pepper, pith and seeds removed and cut into thin strips	1 large red pepper, pith and seeds removed and cut into thin strips
½ cucumber, halved lengthways, seeds removed and cut into 2.5cm./1in. lengths	½ cucumber, halved lengthways, seeds removed and cut into 1in. lengths
4 button mushrooms, sliced	4 button mushrooms, sliced

Heat the oil in a large, deep frying-pan. When it is hot, add the ginger and stir-fry for 2 minutes. Add the leek and carrots and stir-fry for 2 minutes.

Add the remaining ingredients and stir-fry for 3 minutes, or until all the vegetables are just cooked but still crisp.

Serve at once.

Serves 4-6

Preparation and cooking time: 25 minutes

Stir-Fried Broccoli

Metric/Imperial	American
75ml./3fl.oz. sesame oil	⅓ cup sesame oil
1kg./2lb. broccoli, broken into flowerets, then cut on the diagonal into 2cm./1in. lengths	2lb. broccoli, broken into flowerets, then cut on the diagonal into 1in. lengths
1 tsp. salt	1 tsp. salt
½ tsp. sugar	½ tsp. sugar
300ml./10fl.oz. chicken stock	1¼ cups chicken stock
2 tsp. cornflour, mixed to a paste with 1 Tbs. water	2 tsp. cornstarch, mixed to a paste with 1 Tbs. water

Heat the oil in a large saucepan. When it is hot, add the broccoli and stir-fry for 2 minutes.

Add the salt, sugar and chicken stock and stir well. Bring to the boil, cover the pan and cook for 8 minutes, or until the broccoli is cooked but still crisp.

Stir in the cornflour (cornstarch) mixture and cook, stirring constantly, until the sauce thickens and becomes translucent.

Transfer to a warmed serving dish and serve at once.

Serves 6

Preparation and cooking time: 25 minutes

Stir-Braised Cauliflower with Parsley

A delicious dish of Stir-Fried Mixed Vegetables cooked in the traditional Chinese way to keep their goodness and crispness.

Metric/Imperial	American
50ml./2fl.oz. peanut oil	4 Tbs. peanut oil
1 medium cauliflower, broken into flowerets	1 medium cauliflower, broken into flowerets
1 medium onion, chopped	1 medium onion, chopped
1 garlic clove, crushed	1 garlic clove, crushed
½ tsp. ground ginger	½ tsp. ground ginger
¼ tsp. 5-spice powder	¼ tsp. 5-spice powder
150ml./5fl.oz. vegetable or beef stock	⅔ cup vegetable or beef stock
2 Tbs. rice wine or dry sherry	2 Tbs. rice wine or dry sherry
4 Tbs. chopped parsley	4 Tbs. chopped parsley

Heat the oil in a large frying-pan. When it is hot, add the cauliflower, onion, garlic and ginger and stir-fry for 5 minutes. Pour over the stock and wine or sherry, then stir in the parsley.

Bring to the boil, cover the pan and cook the mixture over moderate heat for 7 minutes, stirring occasionally.

Transfer the mixture to a warmed serving dish and serve at once.

Serves 6
Preparation and cooking time: 20 minutes

Ginger, famous for its sweet flavour, is an extremely important cooking ingredient throughout the Orient, used not only in curries and in almost all Chinese recipes, but also as a garnish especially in Japan. If buying fresh, the woody husk should be removed and the yellow, succulent flesh should be sliced or finely chopped before use.

Stir-Fried Spinach with Water Chestnuts

Metric/Imperial	American
50ml./2fl.oz. vegetable oil	$\frac{1}{4}$ cup vegetable oil
50g./2oz. bamboo shoot, sliced	$\frac{1}{4}$ cup sliced bamboo shoot
4 dried mushrooms, soaked in cold water for 30 minutes, drained and sliced	4 dried mushrooms, soaked in cold water for 30 minutes, drained and sliced

Metric/Imperial	American
125g./4oz. water chestnuts, sliced	½ cup water chestnuts, sliced
½kg./1lb. fresh leaf spinach, chopped	2 cups chopped leaf spinach
2 pieces star anise	2 pieces star anise
1 Tbs. oyster sauce	1 Tbs. oyster sauce
1 tsp. sugar	1 tsp. sugar

Heat the oil in a large, deep frying-pan. When it is hot, add the vegetables, except the spinach, and stir-fry for 3 minutes. Add the spinach and remaining ingredients and stir-fry for a further 2 minutes.

Transfer the mixture to a warmed serving dish and serve at once.

Serves 6
Preparation and cooking time: 40 minutes

Gingered Vegetables

Metric/Imperial	American
3 Tbs. peanut oil	3 Tbs. peanut oil
10cm./4in. piece of fresh root ginger, peeled and chopped	4in. piece of fresh green ginger, peeled and chopped
1 leek, white part only, thinly sliced on the diagonal	1 leek, white part only, thinly sliced on the diagonal
1 green pepper, pith and seeds removed and chopped	1 green pepper, pith and seeds removed and chopped
1 red pepper, pith and seeds removed and chopped	1 red pepper, pith and seeds removed and chopped
75g./3oz. bamboo shoots, sliced	½ cup sliced bamboo shoots
125g./4oz. bean sprouts	½ cup bean sprouts
50ml./2fl.oz. chicken stock	¼ cup chicken stock
2 Tbs. soya sauce	2 Tbs. soy sauce
½ tsp. sugar	½ tsp. sugar
2 tsp. cornflour, mixed to a paste with 2 Tbs. water	2 tsp. cornstarch mixed to a paste with 2 Tbs. water

Heat the oil in a large frying-pan. When it is hot, add the ginger and stir-fry for 2 minutes. Stir in the vegetables and stir-fry for 5 minutes. Pour over the stock, soy sauce and sugar, and bring to the boil. Add the cornflour (cornstarch) mixture and cook, stirring constantly, until the sauce thickens and becomes translucent.

Transfer the mixture to a warmed serving dish and serve at once.

Serves 6
Preparation and cooking time: 30 minutes

Bean Sprouts with Green Pepper

Metric/Imperial	American
50ml./2fl.oz. vegetable oil	¼ cup vegetable oil
2 large green peppers, pith and seeds removed and cut into thin strips	2 large green peppers, pith and seeds removed and cut into thin strips

Metric/Imperial	American
1kg./2lb. bean sprouts	4 cups bean sprouts
3 Tbs. rice wine or dry sherry	3 Tbs. rice wine or dry sherry
2 tsp. salt	2 tsp. salt
$\frac{1}{4}$ tsp. monosodium glutamate (optional)	$\frac{1}{4}$ tsp. MSG (optional)

Heat the oil in a large, deep frying-pan. When it is hot, add the peppers and stir-fry for 2 minutes. Add the bean sprouts and stir-fry for a further 2 minutes.

Add the remaining ingredients and stir-fry for 2 minutes. Transfer the mixture to a warmed serving dish and serve at once.

Serves 6-8
Preparation and cooking time: 20 minutes

Quick-Fried Bean Sprouts

Metric/Imperial	American
$\frac{1}{2}$kg./1lb. bean sprouts	2 cups bean sprouts
3 Tbs. sesame oil	3 Tbs. sesame oil
2 spring onions, finely chopped	2 scallions, finely chopped
4 Tbs. Chinese cabbage, finely chopped	4 Tbs. Chinese cabbage, finely chopped
1 tsp. salt	1 tsp. salt
$2\frac{1}{2}$ Tbs. chicken stock	$2\frac{1}{2}$ Tbs. chicken stock

Heat the oil in a large frying-pan. When it is very hot, add the onion and stir-fry for 30 seconds. Stir in the bean sprouts and cabbage and stir-fry until they are translucent. Sprinkle over the salt and stir-fry for a further $1\frac{1}{2}$ minutes. Add the stock and stir-fry for 1 minute.

Transfer to a warmed serving dish and serve.

Serves 4
Preparation and cooking time: 15 minutes

As fresh beansprouts are difficult to obtain, growing your own offers an easy solution: a glass jar, covered with a piece of cheesecloth secured by a rubber band and containing 10ml. (2 teaspoons) of thoroughly rinsed seed, should be put on its side in a dark place and taken out, thereafter, twice daily to be rinsed. The beansprouts will be ready to eat (see right) within a few days and make a nutritious accompaniment to most Chinese meals, as with this dish (far right) of quick-fried beansprouts.

The Chinese seldom eat desserts but Honey Apples, dipped in honey, batter and deep-fried and decorated with icing (confectioners') sugar, is a favourite both within and outside China.

SWEETS

Honey Apples

Metric/Imperial	American
5 medium cooking apples, peeled, cored and cut into 4 rings	5 medium cooking apples, peeled, cored and cut into 4 rings
SYRUP	SYRUP
125g./4oz. soft brown sugar	$\frac{2}{3}$ cup soft brown sugar
4 Tbs. clear honey	4 Tbs. clear honey
250ml./8fl.oz. water	1 cup water
juice of 2 lemons	juice of 2 lemons
BATTER	BATTER
125g./4oz. flour	1 cup flour
$\frac{1}{8}$ tsp. salt	$\frac{1}{8}$ tsp. salt
2 tsp. sugar	2 tsp. sugar
3 egg yolks	3 egg yolks
75ml./6fl.oz. water	$\frac{3}{4}$ cup water
3 egg whites, stiffly beaten	3 egg whites, stiffly beaten
vegetable oil for deep-frying	vegetable oil for deep-frying
DECORATION	DECORATION
75g./3oz. icing sugar	$\frac{3}{4}$ cup confectioners' sugar
1 lemon, sliced	1 lemon, sliced

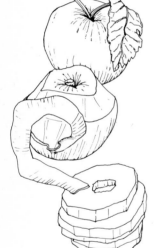

To make the syrup, put the sugar, honey and water in a large saucepan and bring to the boil. Boil for 5 minutes. Remove from the heat and stir in the lemon juice. Drop the apple rings into the syrup and carefully stir to coat them thoroughly. Set aside for 1 hour.

Meanwhile, to make the batter sift the flour and salt into a large bowl. Stir in the sugar. Beat in the egg yolks and water, then fold in the egg whites. Using a slotted spoon, transfer the apple rings to the batter and stir well to coat them completely. Discard the syrup. Set the batter mixture aside.

Fill a large saucepan one-third full with oil and heat until it is hot. Carefully drop in the apple rings, a few at a time, and fry for 2 to 3 minutes, or until they are crisp and golden brown. Remove the apple rings from the pan and drain on kitchen towels.

Put the icing (confectioners') sugar in a deep dish. Dip the apples in the sugar and arrange them on a warmed serving dish. Decorate with the lemon slices and serve at once.

Serves 5
Preparation and cooking time: 1½ hours

Pineapple and Ginger Ice-Cream

Metric/Imperial	American
$\frac{1}{2}$ small fresh pineapple, peeled, cored and cut into chunks (reserve any juice)	$\frac{1}{2}$ small fresh pineapple, peeled, cored, and cut into chunks (reserve any juice)
4 Tbs. rice wine or dry sherry	4 Tbs. rice wine or dry sherry
600ml./1 pint vanilla ice-cream	2½ cups vanilla ice-cream
25g./1oz. candied ginger, chopped	1oz. crystallized ginger, chopped

A sweetmeat stuffed with dates, almonds and finely grated orange rind, Wontons with Almonds and Dates is a delicious, crunchy dessert to serve at the end of a Chinese dinner.

Mix the pineapple juice and rice wine or sherry in a bowl. Add the pineapple chunks and set aside for 10 minutes.

Beat the ice-cream in a serving bowl until it has softened slightly. Gently fold in the pineapple chunks mixture and candied (crystallized) ginger until they are well mixed. Serve at once.

Serves 4-6

Preparation time: 15 minutes

Wontons with Almonds and Dates

Metric/Imperial	American
175g./6oz. stoned dates, finely chopped	1 cup finely chopped pitted dates
50g./2oz. slivered almonds	⅓ cup flaked almonds
2 tsp. sesame seeds	2 tsp. sesame seeds
grated rind of 1 orange	grated rind of 1 orange
2 Tbs. orange-flower water	2 Tbs. orange-flower water
225g./8oz. wonton dough (see page 39), thinly rolled and cut into 36 squares, or 36 bought wonton wrappers	8oz. wonton dough (see page 39), thinly rolled and cut into 36 squares, or bought wonton wrappers
vegetable oil for deep-frying	vegetable oil for deep-frying
2 Tbs. icing sugar	2 Tbs. confectioners' sugar
1 orange, thinly sliced	1 orange, thinly sliced

Put the dates, almonds, sesame seeds, orange rind and orange-flower water in a bowl and knead the mixture until the ingredients are combined.

Lay the wonton wrappers on a flat surface and put a little filling just below the centre. Wet the edges of the dough, then fold over one corner to make a triangle, pinching the edges together to seal. Pull the corners at the base of the triangle together and pinch to seal.

Fill a large saucepan one-third full with oil and heat until it is very hot. Carefully lower the wontons into the oil, a few at a time, and fry for 2 minutes, or until they are golden brown and crisp. Remove from the oil and drain on kitchen towels.

Arrange the cooked wontons on a warmed serving dish. Sprinkle over the icing (confectioners') sugar and garnish with the orange slices. Serve at once.
Serves 4-6
Preparation and cooking time: 25 minutes

Peking Dust

This is a simplified version of a classic dessert; traditionally fresh chestnuts are used and cooked then puréed. In the recipe below the dish is garnished with preserved ginger and almonds, but halved walnuts or kumquats could also be used.

Metric/Imperial	American
300ml./10fl.oz. double cream	1¼ cups heavy cream
150ml./5fl.oz. single cream	⅔ cup light cream
450g./1lb. canned unsweetened chestnut purée	1lb. canned unsweetened chestnut purée
2 Tbs. water	2 Tbs. water
6 whole almonds	6 whole almonds
50g./2oz. preserved ginger, chopped	⅓ cup chopped crystalized ginger

Put the creams into a bowl and beat until they form stiff peaks. Transfer the mixture to a serving dish, piling up into a dome shape.

Beat the purée and water smooth and soft. Using a flat-bladed knife or the back of a spoon, gradually smooth the purée mixture over the cream mixture until it completely encloses it.

Garnish with the almonds and preserved (candied) ginger and serve at once.
Serves 6
Preparation time: 15 minutes

How To Use Chopsticks

Chopsticks, the traditional way of eating Chinese food, adds excitement to Chinese meals. Once mastered, chopsticks contribute much to the authenticity of Chinese luncheons and dinners. These three photographs illustrate the basic stages of eating with chopsticks.

To start, hold one chopstick between thumb and index finger, against the middle and ring fingers.

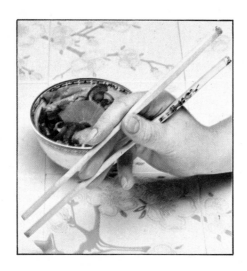

The second chopstick should be placed under the thumb against the index finger.

The final positioning of both chopsticks culminates in picking up the food. The second chopstick should be flexible and able to move easily and should be able to support the food with the first.

GLOSSARY

Bamboo shoot
The cone-shaped shoot of tropical bamboo. It is usually sold canned in the West, packed in water. Leftover bean shoot should be stored in fresh water in the refrigerator, changing water frequently. It will keep for about 2 weeks in this way. Obtainable from any oriental store and most larger supermarkets.

Bean curd
One of the most important products of the soya bean. It is sold fresh, in white, shimmering 'cakes' that look somewhat similar to a soft cheese. Fresh bean curd should be stored in fresh cold water in the refrigerator; it will keep for about 2-3 days. Also available canned, in small cubes. When opened, treat as fresh bean curd. Red bean curd is a variety of the above only sold in cans. It is much stronger and should be used sparingly. Available fresh or canned from oriental stores.

Bean sprouts
Sprouts from the mung bean, a plant which also produces the bean from which soy sauce and bean curd are made. Used extensively in Chinese cooking. Available fresh, usually in plastic packs, or canned. Use the fresh variety if possible. If necessary, use canned but always refresh under cold running water to remove excess salt before adding to recipes. To store, either keep unopened in a plastic bag in the refrigerator or immerse in water, changing daily. They will keep for up to 15 days. Fresh bean sprouts are available from oriental stores and health food shops. Canned from oriental stores and most larger supermarkets.

Black beans
Fermented, heavily salted black beans form an important part of Chinese regional cooking in Szechwan and Canton. Sold in cans and sometimes jars. Refresh under cold running water to remove any excess salt before adding to recipes. To store leftover black beans, put in a covered container and keep in the refrigerator. They will keep for about 6 months. Available from oriental stores.

Cellophane noodles
Fine vermicelli made from the starch of the mung bean. Often require only soaking in hot water before use, although they are sometimes deep-fried. Substitute rice vermicelli if unobtainable. Available only from oriental stores.

Chilli sauce
A popular mixture used throughout Chinese cooking, made from a mixture of chillies, salt and vinegar. Quite hot, so use sparingly. Sold in jars and keeps indefinitely. Obtainable from stores and most supermarkets.

Dried mushrooms
Edible fungi of all types are popular in Chinese cooking. Chinese-type dried mushrooms are black and are usually sold by weight in oriental stores. They will keep for up to 1 year. Always soak for at least 30 minutes, before using, to soften and remove the rather hard, woody stalks if necessary. Do not substitute European dried mushrooms if they are unavailable – the flavour is very different.

Five spice powder
A popular seasoning in Chinese cooking, a mixture of ground cinnamon, cloves, Szechwan pepper, fennel and star anise. It is reddish brown in colour and available from oriental stores. Omit from the recipe if unobtainable, or substitute cloves or allspice.

Ginger
One of the most necessary ingredients in all oriental cooking. Fresh ginger is knobbly and light brown in colour. To use, peel the skin and remove the woody pieces. To store leftover ginger, either wrap tightly, unpeeled, in plastic film or cover with dry sherry. Always store in the refrigerator. Keeps for about six weeks. If fresh ginger is unavailable, ground ginger can be substituted but the taste will be very much inferior. Use about $\frac{1}{2}$ teaspoon ground ginger in place of 4cm./1$\frac{1}{2}$in. piece of fresh (green) ginger. Available from all oriental stores and some specialty vegetable shops.

Hoi Sin sauce
Chinese barbecue sauce, reddish brown in colour and of thick, pouring consistency. Used in cooking as a marinade and sauce thickener and often added as a condiment to cooked food. Keeps indefinitely. Available from oriental stores.

Monosodium glutamate (MSG)
A powder of white crystals, somewhat resembling salt in appearance. Used extensively in both Chinese and Japanese cooking, although its use is somewhat frowned upon in the West. Generally supposed to act as a catalyst for other flavours in a dish, rather than having a strong taste of its own but can easily be omitted from a recipe if you prefer. It is always given as an optional ingredient in this book. Available from supermarkets.

Oyster sauce
Delicate, brownish sauce made from a mixture of oysters and soy sauce. Available in cans or bottles from oriental stores. It will keep indefinitely. No substitute if unobtainable.

Rice vermicelli

A fine, white noodle used extensively throughout China and South-East Asia. Sometime merely soaked in hot water before being used in specific recipes, although it i sometimes deep-fried to make crispy noodles. Available from oriental stores. No substitut – egg vermicelli is very different and should not be substituted in recipes which call fo rice vermicelli.

Soy sauce

A condiment made from fermented soya beans, and one of the staple ingredients i Chinese, Japanese, Korean and South-East Asian cooking. Always use Chinese soy sauc for Chinese food. Light soy sauce is used basically for white meat and fish, dark, heavie soy sauce for dark meats. Stores indefinitely in the bottle or jar. Available from supe markets and oriental stores.

Star anise

Pretty, black 8-pointed star shaped spice, which is used quite frequently in Chines cooking. Available from oriental stores. If unavailable, omit from the recipe – there i no substitute.

Water chestnuts

Small white bulbs, usually available canned in the West. To store, put leftover wate chestnuts in a covered container in the refrigerator, changing the water frequently. The will keep for about 1 month. Available from oriental stores and better supermarkets.

RECIPE INDEX

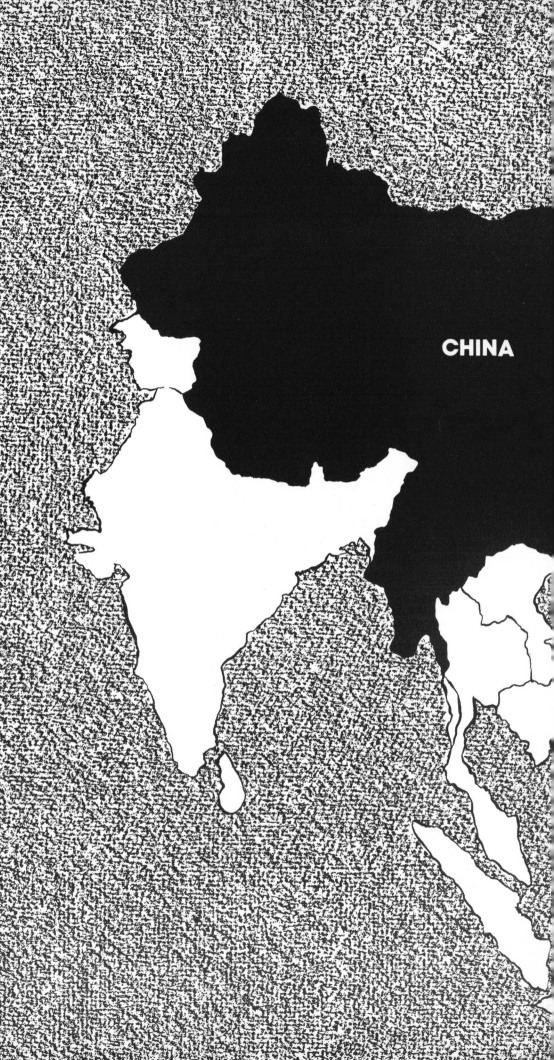